JUAN-MARIA
GALLEGO-TOLEDO

THE
SHADOW
OF BIAS
How to Improve Your Team's
Productivity and Performance
Through Inclusion
ON LEADERSHIP

*The Shadow of Bias on Leadership: How to improve your team's
productivity and performance through inclusion*

Copyright © 2019 Juan-Maria Gallego-Toledo, PsyD

Print ISBN: 978-1-54-397464-5

eBook ISBN: 978-1-54-397465-2

Library of Congress Control Number: 2019906514

Front Cover Image: Jesús Gallego Toledo

First printing edition 2019.

TABLE OF CONTENTS

INTRODUCTION

This book has been in the making for the past decade. I have been fascinated with culture since my parents enlisted me as a three-year-old child in a French school in Spain. I soon discovered that what worked with some of my French teachers did not work with my Spanish teachers. For example, French teachers expected their students to push back on their ideas, ask questions, and be curious. My Spanish teachers saw those acts as disrespectful. I enjoyed conversations with some friends, and others, I could not understand where they were coming from. Like, why would someone not eat pork? I mean, deli meats such as chorizo or *jamón serrano* were the best things in the world.

Then I started spending my summers in Cork, Ireland, and I could not understand why certain simple ideas were so controversial to my Irish "mom" but logical to my French roommate. For example, the need to separate religion from the government was a foreign concept to my devout Catholic Irish mom but an acceptable one for both my French roommate and me. Moreover, moving to Walled Lake, Michigan, a suburb outside of Detroit, was a major eye-opening experience when my normal behaviors were questioned by my high school peers and by my American "parents." Why couldn't all these people be more normal? But then, what's normal? Is my normal universal?

During my professional career, I worked as a global sales and marketing executive in Latin America, Europe, Morocco, China, and the United States. During my last assignment with Nokia (a Finnish telecommunications manufacturer), I spent over two years working in Beijing, China, as an expat. I led strategy and sales development for the China Mobile account team, the largest mobile operator in the world.

One of my responsibilities was to train the account's regional sales directors at Nokia on coaching. At the time, Nokia expected all its leaders to coach and mentor most of their direct reports as a developmental tool, establishing a possible succession plan as well. Shared leadership, flat structures, and effective teamwork were part of the Finnish approach to leading a business unit. I welcomed that aspect of the Nokia culture as refreshing and uplifting developmental challenge. It was a sign of Nokia´s commitment to its employees´ professional growth. I aligned with the concept that a leader needs to develop other leaders and make him or herself obsolete. When we spend too much time in the same position, we lose our fresh ideas and, therefore, lose competitiveness.

In 2008, I started a new sales development project in Beijing, China. I was asked to train our top account sales executives on a specific coaching technique used in the organization. I had previously used this method among sales executives in other parts of Europe and Latin America to various levels of success. The idea was simple— get the executives to use the coaching technique to develop the next generation of sales executive leaders. Imagine my frustration when after two and a half years, I had only successfully trained two of the six Chinese executives.

Furthermore, I was exasperated at my inability to convey the benefits of coaching one´s direct reports. After a year on the job, I noticed a passive resistance to the program. Directors would come to my developmental meetings or would welcome me to their regional offices, but suddenly, their direct reports would have a mysterious meeting and could not participate in the workshop. I only had half of my audience, a challenging situation since I had only potential coaches but no one to coach.

As I pushed for implementation, the resistance became more active and evident, not just from the sales directors but from my new direct-line supervisor. Despite arguing the need to align with the Nokia organizational culture and sharing the evidence supporting the benefits of coaching and its positive effects on productivity and job satisfaction, I was unable to change my colleagues' mindset. My logical arguments failed to build the necessary support for the project. I failed to understand an important part of the Chinese business culture—controlling knowledge meant job security. Subsequently, I realized that something was missing in my arguments. I could not reach those capable individuals, and I could not understand why.

This frustrating curiosity only grew during my first consulting project. Shortly after I left Nokia to complete my doctoral work, I was asked to consult on a project for a Madrid-based company with operations in Latin America and Spain. I met with the company's board of directors, who requested help developing alternative sources of revenue for the private company. The company had a sole source of revenue and wanted to diversify with possible plans to go public in a couple of years. Thinking back to the day that I accepted that project, I kick myself for not listening to the words of warning from one of the directors, a former customer and good friend, who warned me that "I would not enjoy working in that company." But I was optimistic about the company's revenue potential and about my ability to make it happen. Alas, I filtered the negative warning, and I focused on other colleagues' comments supporting my participation in the project. The "they need you badly" remarks played well to my professional ego and, therefore, I accepted the project. I ignored the contradicting information, concentrated on the positive information

only, and confirmed my decision with the one-sided supporting information—a perfect example of optimism and confirmation bias.[1]

However, after three months, I could not wait for the project
to be over. The new revenue generating ideas that my team and I
were proposing were constantly rejected. We were pushed to support the company's traditional operations. I soon realized that the
new revenue streams the executive board expected were the same
no-risk ventures that already existed—a logistics and finance opera-
tion with minimal capital investment risk. Therefore, my other diversi-
fying efforts were not supported by all board members. Projects were
expected to be revenue neutral or positive from the first month and
involve minimal financial risk for the company. There was a clear mis-
alignment between my personal and professional values and those
of the organization and its leadership. Our definitions of risk were
completely misaligned. One of the directors sabotaged a potential project that a colleague suggested, and I supported, strongly
believing that it could bring in significant revenue. That was the straw
that broke the camel's back. We mutually agreed to part with three
months left on the contract.

Likewise, several years later another realization hit me during
a certification course on Leader Network Diagnostic run by a colleague, Phil Willburn, at the Center for Creative Leadership, one of
the leading nonprofit executive training institutions, ranked in the
top ten in the *Financial Times* for worldwide executive education.
During the workshop, I realized how easy it is for leaders to fall into the
groupthink trap, that's the tendency to support the most common
idea or the perceived expert's idea, without considering all angles.
Groupthink reduces creativity and increases the likelihood of fundamental errors in groups by discouraging disagreements. Individual

---

1   Tali Sharot, "The Optimism Bias," *Current Biology* 21, no. 23 (2011): R941–R945.

contributors refrain from expressing dissenting concerns from a team member's idea—normally, the person perceived as the leader (hierarchical leader, expert, senior employee, etc.).

During that workshop, we learned to evaluate how open or close one´s network is within an organization and to consider all the potential bias traps related to the closeness of our network. A network's level of closeness and openness is defined by the members' existing connections—the more connections you have, the higher the network's level of closeness. The lower the level of connections, the more open the network is.

Another idea of Willburn's Leader Network Diagnostic is that our network should evolve along with our professional development and career advancements to capitalize on the expertise and individual contacts within that evolving network. As leaders, we should aim to have as open a network as possible for optimal access to fresh, and even conflicting information. Dissenting ideas are necessary elements of a team's creativity. We should seek a diverse array of professionals inside and outside of our organization (or even industry) to expand our knowledge of different environments and perspectives. A closed network is like pushing your car's air recycling button—yes, it may help keep the car warmer or colder and save energy, but no fresh air is getting in. A closed network takes our ideas, recycles them through the same group of people and comes back to us to reinforce the "fact" that we were right, and we had a great idea. Networks should invite new perspectives to enrich our context and prevent the dangers of groupthink. In addition to the limited number of people in your network, you could create an artificial closeness by limiting the type of individuals you have surrounded yourself with. Connections with the same educational, social, or cultural backgrounds, for example, could mimic the effects of a close network.

On the other hand, everything I just told you about is simple human nature. As humans, we want to be close to people like us, people who agree with us, make us feel safer, smarter, and appreciated. Social acceptance is one of our goals in life because humans are social animals. And as business leaders, we believe that we were put into our position to lead, to provide answers to any question, to come up with the best solution to a problem. After all, leaders should have an answer, right? As consultants, we would answer "not necessarily."

An inclusive leader is an individual with an awareness of her biases. She prevents them from affecting her decision-making process, invites different points of view, and establishes a psychologically safe environment for her teams. It is a leader who uses critical thinking to come up with the best solutions to an issue within a multicultural environment, with the right balance of empathy and factual detachment. It is a person aware of her social identity (values, beliefs, and mores), who is knowledgeable about how those elements affect her perceptions, emotions, and judgment or filter her message to others. An inclusive leader improves collaboration and leadership through exposure to diverse group members and by developing processes to neutralize organizational biases. In these ways, inclusive leaders motivate employees to peak performance, driving productivity and profitability to new highs. Inclusively leading our diverse workforce not only improves our organization's performance, but it makes our community and society stronger.

My passion for diversity, inclusion, and leadership has pushed me to focus my research over the last five years on finding how to become a better, more inclusive leader in this complex world. As one part of my research, I have read articles and books about the effects of biases on leaders' decision-making processes. Many leadership studies reveal unconscious bias. For example, when I studied about personality, I learned about the concept of autopilot, the most energy-efficient and comfortable way in which to operate. When I looked at different leadership and 360 assessments, I discovered that all of us have hot buttons, derailers, and triggers—attributes that can push us over the edge, reduce our productivity, and potentially drive us in the wrong direction.

Anyone who works globally learns quickly that different cultures require different leadership styles. An American manager cannot go into a Japanese company and ignore the need for consensus during the decision-making process. A frank and direct Dutch director might not understand why her Chinese team fails to speak up during meetings. We know we are all different people; still, we pay little attention to the way we formulate our decisions and the role that unconscious bias plays in our successes and failures as leaders.

Let me give you an example. First of all, allow me to make a confession - I do have a predisposition to react energetically to challenging situations. As a teenager, this was manifested with slammed doors and lots of yelling. I did become aware that this attitude was not helping me much and was starting to isolate me from friends and family. I decided to change my approach. Now, when something irritates me, I give it about ten seconds during which time I evaluate solutions and I ask myself "why is this so important to me?". Before, I used to jump into introspective problem solving, and then my first words were potential solutions. For many years, I headed a sales and marketing team in Latin America. On this particular Spring Texas day, I was sitting in my office, when one of my best sales managers (and good friend) walked into my office freaked out about a recent event affecting our sales in Colombia. He spoke vigorously, loudly, with plenty of hand gestures. I listened and started to make a mental list of pros and cons, and during a brief break in his talking, I suggested we analyze the different approaches to the challenge.

He stopped talking and looked at me. "No," he said.

"What do you mean *no*?" I replied, amused.

"No, you cannot jump into solution mode until you understand how this is affecting me and your team."

My approach to keep calm and effective had lacked social awareness. I suggested that he step out of my office and walk back in as if it was the first time that we had seen each other that morning. He went out and came back yelling and complaining. I allowed myself to freak out with him for about one minute, and then I suggested that we start working on a solution. He smiled and said, "Let's get to it."

Acknowledging his pain predisposed him to seek solutions. From there on, I still paused when faced with an irritating situation, but now, I put myself first in the shoes of my employee, client, spouse, daughter, friend, and then, after I empathize with the individual, we start working on solutions.

I wrote this book with two major assumptions in mind. The first one is that developing a diverse team could present serious challenges that may not be found in homogeneous teams. Remember Tuckman's model for the development of teams? It stated that teams go through a four-stage process: forming, storming, norming, and performing. During the forming stage, everyone is nice to each other because they want to fit in and be liked. You are evaluating the other people. Then you jump into the storming phase, where conflict finally appears. You feel comfortable arguing with each other. Not much gets done, but some would say this stage is where creativity resides. Finally, a set of rules are established and possibly a process defined to accomplish the goal. The team is able to address the challenge (problem or opportunity) at hand. Yes, the norming and forming phases of the group creation and the decision-making process may be a bit more challenging in a diverse group, but the overall results, the quality of the output is usually better than fairly homogeneous groups.

McKinsey Consulting, the Boston Consulting Group, Deloitte Consulting LLP, and major universities have supporting research for the importance of diversity in teams. Studies conclude that diverse teams contribute to output quality, profitability, and productivity for the organization. Researchers from Stanford and the University of Chicago concluded that 25 percent of US economic growth between 1960 and 2010 resulted from women and minorities access-ing high-skill jobs through better hiring practices and shifting employer attitudes, access to education, and changes in regulations.[2]

The second assumption is that we all have implicit and con-scious biases that affect how we filter input during our decision-mak-ing processes. As Anna Laszlo, the director of Fair and Impartial Policing, stated during a 2015 interview, "The science tells [us] that if [we] hire from the human race, [we're] going to be hiring biased individuals...."[3]

Over the next pages, I will address two perspectives: the behavioral or self-awareness aspect of the leader and the structural or procedural systems that will prevent those biases from influencing management decisions. We will tackle potential solutions for how to best manage those biases as leaders operating in a complex and multicultural world. We will start with the task of making the implicit

---

2 Dan Kopf, "Fifty Years of Economic History Proves that Inclusive Workplaces Make Us All Richer," Quartz at Work, August 30, 2018, https://qz.com/work/1372277/fifty-years-of-economic-history-proves-that-inclusive-workplaces-make-us-all-richer/
Chang-Tai Hsieh, Erik Hurst, Charles I. Jones, Peter J. Klenow, "The Allocation of Talent and U.S. Economic Growth," (working paper, The National Bureau of Economic Research, April 8, 2018), http://klenow.com/HHJK.pdf.

3 S.G. Carmichael, "Training Police Departments to Be Less Biased," *Harvard Business Review Digital Articles*, (2015): 3.

explicit through self-awareness, one of the four components of emotional intelligence. We will also look at different research-based techniques to minimize the impact of biases on our decisions and support an inclusive organizational culture.

Regardless of the type of leadership that we practice, we must learn to address the shadows of our biases in our daily decisions. We need to understand their effects on our partners, customers, employees, and other stakeholders. And these decisions go beyond the workplace to our families, communities, and social interactions. For example, prejudices will show in the way we behave when we participate in our children´s teacher-parent conferences. They will show when we are in the checkout line at the grocery store. They will creep in when we travel for business or leisure.

After all, we should understand that our professional leadership responsibilities extend to our behaviors outside the workplace. With the ever-presence of social media and smartphones, we need to be at our best while representing our employer during business hours as well as outside them. I hope that the techniques presented in this book will facilitate the context-acceptable behaviors.

To conclude this introduction, let me provide you with some details on how we will fulfill our journey toward greater self-awareness and our potential transformation into an unbiased (or less biased) leader. The book will include a theoretical section, which will cover the challenges of the complexity we face in our day-to-day lives. We will tackle two different types of complexities: Human Complexity and the Global Business Complexity. To better understand these, I will introduce some relevant background research and theories behind the things we do, the psychological and biological reasons we do them, and why we need to change. Then, we will tackle different approaches to manage that complexity. I will provide methods to improve your emotional intelligence and set organizational processes to prevent or minimize the effects of biases so you can optimize the use of diverse teams.

We will learn about the complexities of the multicultural business world that force us to become the leaders of shape-shifting organizations. I will summarize some past research on dominant cultures and how cognitive decisions are made, introducing the bias-centered error. Don´t worry! I will keep it short, giving you the basic information without sinking into the academic theoretical black hole. I will introduce the different and most suitable techniques to improve our cultural self-awareness and establish the structure and procedures within your organization to minimize the influence of those biases as much as possible. These techniques will move you forward in your journey toward becoming a more inclusive leader.

In the practical side of the book, I will present research-supported techniques that I have learned over my twenty-five plus years of global experience working with different cultures in United States, Latin America, Europe, Morocco, and China. I have incorporated many of those techniques in my diversity and inclusion training to law enforcement agencies in Colorado and through my volunteer work facilitating dialogue among the community and local law enforcement departments.

While I will simplify many concepts, I will provide you with plenty of references in the footnotes to expand on any topics that you may want to delve deeper into in your own time. Of course, the footnotes are also a way to give credit to those authors and researchers that have done the hard work. I am not reinventing the wheel here but simply consolidating some of the most relevant research on bias and prejudice in leadership, adding my own business experiences as the thread to bring it all together in the most practical way possible.

You need to understand that there is a reading bias that may cause me to focus on certain information while ignoring other bits that may be as important. As I read hundreds of books and articles, I probably felt into the trap of favoring and choosing data to confirm my own perspective on this matter, despite my efforts to remain as impartial as possible. I would urge you to read any of the sources and come to your own conclusions. And feel free to reach out to me with your interpretations (juan.m.gallego@selfmetanoia.com). And feel free to follow the updates in my blog https://medium.com/the-journey-towards-leaders-inclusiveness.

I hope that you enjoy the book as much as I enjoyed writing it.

Juan M.ª Gallego Toledo, PsyD

Colorado Springs, Colorado

April 29, 2019

PART I

THE CHALLENGE OF HUMAN COMPLEXITY

HUMAN COMPLEXITY

How Our Reptilian Brain Interferes with Our Leadership

A recent report written by Citigroup and Oxford University and mentioned by the *Financial Times* found that two-thirds of US GDP growth since 2011 could be attributed to the activities of immigrants. Supported by statistical analysis and extensive research, the report argued that freezing the immigration rates would negatively affect the overall GDP in the United States.[4]

Faced with a recent influx of illegal immigration from the Middle East and Africa, Western European countries' biggest political argument against immigration revolves around the pressure on the (already-strained) welfare systems. However, that's not the case in the United States since the country offers a minimal social safety net compared to all other developed countries, is regulated by flexible labor rules, and currently (2018) enjoys a historically low unemployment rate. Economists have established that any migrant would actually be a net contributor to the public finances[5] and the overall economy. What's more, there is a shortage of skilled labor in the United States that could negatively affect future economic growth and push consumer prices up[6] with a detrimental effect on the country's inflation rate.

---

4 Benjamin Fearnow, "Immigrants Account for Two-Thirds of US Economic Growth Since 2011, Analysis Finds," *Newsweek*, September 9, 2018, https://www.newsweek.com/migrants-immigration-1113006.

5 *The Economist*, "The Way Forward on Immigration to the West," August 25, 2018, https://www.economist.com/leaders/2018/08/25/the-way-forward-on-immigration-to-the-west.

6 Jeff Cox, "The U.S. Labor Shortage Is Reaching a Critical Point," *CNBC*, July 5, 2018, https://www.cnbc.com/2018/07/05/the-us-labor-shortage-is-reaching-a-critical-point.html.

What about the increasing crime rate that some politicians attribute to immigrants? Government statistics show a steady decline in violent crime in most large American cities. According to data collected by the Marshall Project, while immigration has been growing dramatically over the past twenty-five years, the percentage of violent crime has decreased nationally by 36 percent over the same period.[7] Studies conducted by criminologists documented that crimes in the United States are less likely to be committed by immigrants than by US-born citizens.[8] Finally, a recent government report found that the United States' birth rates are at their lowest level in thirty years,[9] meaning that current generations are not having enough children to replace themselves. Additionally, most Western economies are facing an aging population and declining tax contributions to social security programs. My question to my readers is: should we accept more immigrants to feed the current economic growth in the United States?

The chances that these statistics shifted anyone´s opinion are minimal. Studies show that statistics are necessary to uncover the truth about a phenomenon or event, but they are not sufficient to change people´s beliefs.[10] If we stay away from the theories alleging biological differences in the brains of liberals and conservatives,[11] the mainstream research argues that statistical information fails to appease our human nature and has minimal impact on our motivation, needs,

---

7   Anna Flagg, "The Myth of the Criminal Immigrant," *The Marshall Project*, March 30, 2018, https://www.themarshallproject.org/2018/03/30/the-myth-of-the-criminal-immigrant.

8   Michael T. Light and Ty Miller, "Does Undocumented Immigration Increase Violent Crimes?" *Criminology* 56, no. 2 (2018): 370–401.

9   Mike Stobbe, "U.S. Birth Rate Plummets to Lowest Point in 30 Years," *USA Today*, May 17, 2018, https://www.usatoday.com/story/news/nation-now/2018/05/17/birth-rate-u-s-drops-fertility-millennials-immigrants/618422002/.

10   Tali Sharot, *The Influential Mind: What the Brain Reveals about Our Power to Change Others* (New York: Henry Holt and Company, 2017).

11   John R. Hibbing, Kevin B. Smith, and John R. Alford, *Predisposed: Liberals, Conservatives, and the Biology of Political Differences* (Routledge, 2013).

beliefs, hopes, and values. If we already believed that immigration could have a positive effect on the economy and is good for our country, then we most likely used motivated reasoning to reinforce our opinion—we pick the facts and figures that support our preconceived ideas. If, on the other hand, we disagreed that immigration is good for the country, we probably questioned the one-sided statistics presented—"obviously, this is the view of one of those liberal college professors"—or we may be questioning some other aspect not mentioned here such as the effects of immigrants on the US culture, the English language, future political policies—that's also motivated reasoning.

Psychological Hijackers

Psychological hijackers are those cognitive events that take over our logical reasoning, reducing the ability to use the brain's frontal lobe, usually kicking us into emotional interpretations and decisions. Those cognitive events are the brain's parallel to the muscle reflex. Something happens, and our autopilot kicks in, nullifying any potential System 2 thinking—the slow, rigorous, controlled, arduous, and attention-demanding thinking process.

Cognitive dissonance is one of the main hijackers. It is related to motivated reasoning, previously mentioned. This term was first introduced by Leon Festinger.[12] We choose (consciously and unconsciously) to filter and interpret the elements of a situation through a series of factors (for example, our relationship to the person speaking, the familiar or unfamiliar surrounding conditions of the presentation, our physiological state...) tainting the psychological meaning of those facts.

---

12   Leon Festinger, "Cognitive Dissonance," *Scientific American* 207, no. 4 (1962): 93–106.

We all suffer from confirmation bias. That is the tendency to select and collect information, to prejudicially interpret it and, finally, unreliably recall it.[13] When we cite facts and statistics to counter another person's belief, we usually elicit a phenomenon called "the backfire effect," pushing the other person to take a more extreme position, strongly supporting his original beliefs, and we fail to bring them closer to our point of view.

Imagine that you believe that the earth is flat. An internet search would reveal thousands of pseudo-scientific sources that demonstrate that the earth is flat and that pictures taken from space are just an illusion. Arguing with an individual who believes this would only result in an exchange of data and push each individual deeper into their beliefs. It would not change either person's mind. Experience is one of the few things that can change someone's values.

I read a story once about Dick Cheney and his negative perception of the LGBTQ community. When his daughter came out as lesbian, suddenly, Mr. Cheney changed his view. He knew his daughter, and he also knew that she did not match all his previous beliefs of what an individual belonging to the LGTBQ community was like. His values and beliefs underwent an experiential shift.

When we meet people from different cultures, we compare foreign, ambiguous, or complex elements with our own experiences. We try to establish similarities between those elements that we understand and the new ones. Let me give you some example on how this works.

For example, based on our previous experiences eating at Chinese restaurants in our home countries, we may notice that we are offer chopsticks to eat with. If we go to China, we may take our experience of eating with chopsticks as a given in that country.

---

13 Marshall Goldsmith and Mark Reiter, *Triggers: Creating Behavior That Lasts— Becoming the Person You Want to Be* (Crown Business, 2015).

Let me offer an example of my own past experience with anchoring. During my time at Central Michigan University, I met several people that had spent vacations in Spain. Automatically, they assumed that I was a smoker and I loved to party because those were the type of Spaniards that they had interacted with during their visit. I also ran into individuals that were convinced we rode horses in Spain and, hence, I was a good horse rider. I have never ridden a horse in my life, but many people connect horses with Spain. Maybe something to do with the conquistadores introducing horses in the Americas...

All these are examples of anchoring. Our brains want to connect the unknown to the familiar and try to explain the ambiguous using our cadre of known facts and opinions, hence, confirming and supporting our existing perception, and most likely, rejecting new ideas or explanations outside it. By the way, breaking those normal anchoring patterns is a technique used in many horror movies. The victims finally feel safe in their own home then suddenly realize that the villain is in the house. Or the little innocent child that suddenly becomes the horrendous creature. Challenging those familiar anchors results in panic and confusion.

In the immigration scenario that I mentioned at the beginning, if our beliefs are anchor to the idea that immigration improves our country, then those facts are perceived as confirming facts. If, on the other hand, we believe that immigration damages our country, then we will find a way to explain those numbers to support our views. And, let me point out an interesting study that suggests that the more educated we are, the more likely we are to err on the side of cognitive dissonance and motivated reasoning and seek to confirm what we already believe. It is hard to break the cognitive dissonance cycle and escape those psychological hijackers, but it is not an impossible task.

Cognitive dissonance is a funny thing. It either helps justify misalignments between an individual's beliefs and actions or it produces discomfort because we know what we're doing goes against what we believe. As Festinger found during his research, we eventually face two possibilities—readjust our values or resist and flee. For example, at work, when faced with some of our managers' decisions that we believe are unethical, we might change our values to adjust to our environment. Those thought elements that we first believed to be, for example, unethical, suddenly could be justified. Or we might resist, becoming a cynic, disengaging from the company and eventually (hopefully) leaving for another company whose organizational values are more aligned with our own.

Likewise, the moral foundation theory supported by Jon Haidt and Jesse Graham argues that moral universals are rooted in *intuitive ethics*. This notion argues that humans are equipped with a set of innate psychological mechanisms that automatically trigger an emotionally based response to the physical, psychological, and social situations we face.

We attach emotions to everything we encounter in our daily lives. Those emotions can be positive or negative and can be perceived as rational, but that may not always be the case. This is why so many smells are connected to memories and emotions. Every time I smell burning alcohol, for example, I get flashbacks to the home visits of María Luisa, the nurse that came to our home to give us vaccines. She would burn the needles in a little tin full of alcohol to disinfect them before giving us the shots. When we smelled the burning alcohol, we knew that pain was coming.

One of my favorite authors is Daniel Kahneman, the 2002 Nobel Prize winner of economic sciences and author of *Thinking, Fast and Slow*.[14] I enjoy the way he conveys and connects his research through his personal experiences, humanizing complex psychological and economic topics. Kahneman illustrates how science affects human behavior in a humorous, simple, and direct manner. Reading his work, I feel as if science is personal to him, part of who he is. His work with Amos Tversky on Prospect Theory in 1974 sets the foundation for behavioral economics, one of my professional interests as a consultant, marketer, and psychologist.

In his early work with Tversky, Kahneman identified three heuristics (mental operations) of judgment: representativeness—used to determine probability under uncertain conditions; availability—making a judgment based on how easy it is to remember something; and anchoring—relying heavily on experiences or an initial bit of information before making a decision. He also identified dozens of systematic biases related to those heuristics that affect our intuitive assessments and predictions, in particular, when making a decision under uncertain conditions.[15]

To summarize this amazing paper, Kahneman and Tversky argued that in uncertainty, individuals rely on these limited heuristics to reduce a complex situation into simple parts, calculate the odds of each potential choice, and come up with the best decisions. And, while those mental operations may be useful, they usually result in "severe and systematic errors" according to Kahneman and Tversky. This is evident in infants and toddlers as they learn about their surroundings. When a toddler throws a toy on the floor and waits for you

14 Daniel Kahneman, *Thinking, Fast and Slow* (New York: Farrar, Straus, and Giroux, 2011).

15 Amos Tversky and Daniel Kahneman, "Judgment under Uncertainty: Heuristics and Biases," *Science* 185, no. 4157 (1974): 1124–1131, http://www.dtic.mil/dtic/tr/fulltext/u2/767426.pdf.

to pick it up, he is doing so because you previously picked up the toy, and he has anchored the behavior with an interaction with you. "I throw the toy, and he pays attention to me." The toddler actions are very smart. The severe and systematic error comes from the adult to pick up the toy, ignoring the Antecent (the context) and without connecting the behavior to the future consequence.

We are bad at calculating statistical probabilities. We are not good at interpreting data and coming up with the appropriate solution.[16] An example of ignoring the odds was the use of exsanguination, or bloodletting, in sick individuals. This is practice started with the Greek physicians who believed sickness would leave the body through the blood. A physician would bleed a person to let the illness out of his system. If the sickness prevailed, the physician would assume he had not let enough blood out. Today we understand that bloodletting reduces the chances of survival, further stressing the system and making the patient even weaker to fight the disease. If, when physicians were practicing bloodletting, would have look at the data, how many people survived a disease without any bloodletting versus with people that did not survive despite the bloodletting, they would have noticed that the chances of survival increased when the good doctor did not interfere with the disease. Statistics would have revealed that bloodletting was killing more people than taking no action.

When we rely on our gut feeling for solutions, we usually make the situation worse and seldom incorporate the correct data for the analysis. Let's ask ourselves, how often do we, as leaders, make decisions about complex matters under uncertainty?

---

16   Alan Smith, April 2016, "Why We Should Love Statistics," a TEDxExeter talk, http://www.ted.com/talks/alan_smith_why_we_re_so_bad_at_statistics.

WE ALL HAVE BIASES

We all have biases. It is a part of our humanity, the way our brains work, the trick to surviving for so many million years. As social animals, we depend on other people for survival, and that dependence is built on a common culture, defined as a set of social rules, norms, values, and beliefs that facilitate the cohabitation, cooperation, and communication. Culture is necessary for social understanding of behaviors. As the quote wrongly attributed to Charles Darwin goes, "[I]t is not the strongest of the species that survives, nor the most intelligent that survives. It is the one that is most adaptable to change."[17]

Every day, we adapt to the changing patterns of people's behaviors within our context, in our corporate and personal environments. This adaptation occurs when we react to new external pressures and a long list of complex and ambiguous factors. Think about how an American organization with European operations based in the UK would have reacted to the results of the Brexit referendum – a decision was made to establish the European headquarters in the UK, part of the European Union, for whatever reason, and then suddenly, this organization is faced with the potential exclusion of the European market. How should that company react to a situation that has never previously happened? A complex and ambiguous political and economic situation that requires an urgent corporate adaptation.

A cognitive pattern is a logical schema such as a pattern of behaviors, or occurrences that is repeated. Studies have shown that we may recognize a pattern at the unconscious level without even trying—our brains love to find connections between things. When

---

17 According to Nicholas Matzke, this quote came from Mr. Leon C. Megginson from Louisiana State University in 1963: https://www.darwinproject.ac.uk/people/about-darwin/six-things-darwin-never-said/evolution-misquotation.

those patterns are based on half-truths or erroneous information, we develop a bias. Researchers tell us that we are prone to develop unconscious (and conscious) habits that facilitate our lives in a quick and recurring manner.[18] It only takes a few repetitions for the brain's basal ganglia to notice and establish a pattern.

Those patterns could be motivated by our social exposure to different cultural practices. Our expectations are partially determined by our cultures, including norms set by our immediate tribe or in-group. Those expectations can act as filters that help us classify things as *normal* or *outside of our normal*, aka wrong. Psychologists Bandura and Vygotsky argued that a child´s exposure to a specific environment and group of people would affect a child's personality and develop the child's concept of culture, ergo, the expectations of that child regarding social patterns,[19] to be read at repeated social behaviors. Patterns help us function in a more effective and energy-saving way. When something breaks the normal pattern, a red flag goes up, and we pay more attention. Those interruptions in the normal pattern are perceived as a challenge to our set of values. Let me give you an example – when large retailers in Spain proposed opening the stores on Sundays, they encountered a strong opposition from small retailers as well as the consumers – "Sundays are meant to be days of rest, family and worship". That proposal was challenging the normal cultural practice at the time. Large retailers had to change certain labor laws and introduce the practice gradually to show that open stores on Sundays did not interfere with family time or worshiping time.

---

18   Charles Duhigg, *The Power of Habit: Why We Do What We Do in Life and Business* (Random House, 2012); David T. Neal, Wendy Wood, and Jeffrey M. Quinn, "Habits—A Repeat Performance," *Current Directions in Psychological Science* 15, no. 4 (2006): 198–202.

19   James C. Goodwin, *A History of Modern Psychology*, (Wiley, 2015).

From a more general perspectives, you may be asking yourself why do we need patterns? The reason mainly lies with the limits of our conscious mind, the things that we can pay full attention and work with logically.

Depending on the book or research you read,[20] the conscious mind governs about 1 percent to 10 percent of our actions at any given moment. In other words, we are mostly unaware of about 90 percent to 99 percent of our actions. And we should be thankful for this because otherwise we would be exhausted physically and mentally. For example, we are not aware of breathing (unless we've over-exerted or are meditating), digestion (unless we ate something wrong or new), walking (unless we are walking through rugged terrain), or such things as sounds or movement in our surroundings (unless we are in a new environment such as a safari through the Serengeti or walking into our new boss's office). And do notice the *unless* statements. When a pattern is broken by something new, our awareness is engaged, leaving the autopilot of unconsciousness, seeking new information about the situation to provide us with additional safety, and seamlessly trying to establish a new pattern to go back to our preferred energy saving mode.[21]

Optimizing our Limited Conscious Bandwidth

Physiologically speaking, patterns help us focus on the *stuff* that matters at that moment. Maybe we are preparing a presentation for a customer, or maybe we are watching our daughter at a school play, or maybe we are studying for an exam or preparing for a speech. Whatever the reason, our frontal cortex, the part of our brain

20 Two of my favorite research-based books on this topic are Jonathan Haidt's *The Righteous Mind: Why Good People Are Divided by Politics and Religion* (Vintage, 2012), and D. Kahneman's *Think, Fast and Slow* (New York: Farrar, Straus and Giroux, 2013).

21 D. Rock, "Managing with the Brain in Mind," *Strategy+Business*, 56 (Autumn 2009): https://www.strategy-business.com/article/09306?gko=5df7f.

that handles logical decisions, critical thinking, mathematical calculations, and mindfulness is a powerful tool with limited bandwidth. Have you ever tried to follow a conversation with your daughter, son, spouse, or friend when something interesting is on the television? Or how much of your back home or to work do you remember when you are talking to someone over the phone (handsfree, of course) or going over the conversation you had with your boss? Have you ever been sitting at a meeting when suddenly everyone goes quiet, all eyes are on you, and you suddenly realize, "Holy Toledo, they just asked me a question!"? By the way, a tip on how to manage that situation successfully without showing your hand is by saying, "Before I share my opinion, I would like to hear what my colleagues have to say on that matter" and cross your fingers that someone was paying attention and that her answer will help you figure out the question.

To optimize our limited conscious bandwidth, our brain relies on patterns. Some of those patterns are learned early on. As an infant, we soon realize that when we cry, someone will most likely take care of the uncomfortable (hunger, pain, fear, or physical discomfort such as a full diaper).

As a child, we may develop other useful patterns. Saying that beets make us nauseous is a quick solution not to have to eat them. Crying or complaining about how hard homework usually earns us a parent's help and attention. Doing a task that our parents asked us to do incorrectly usually makes that task go away.

As we get older, we adapt our survival patterns to match our needs. Those patterns are developed based on a stimulus-response association for the most part. Something happens (a trigger or antecedent) that solicits a certain behavior from us. That behavior gets rewarded or punished by an external response or actor (the consequence). This is known as the A-B-C—the Antecedent (trigger),

Behavior, and Consequence(s) relationship. We repeat the behaviors that give the same desired response, and this is how behavioral patterns are created.[22]

We also create other patterns called fixed programs (routines) to manage our time effectively, such as going to bed and waking up at the same time to get ready for school or work (and hopefully getting your seven to eight hours of needed sleep) or eating the same food for breakfast, which saves us time in the morning. I once heard that US President Barak Obama used to wear the same color suit every day to avoid wasting time choosing a suit in the morning. Driving a certain route to school, work, the airport, or to the relatives' house (maybe a longer one if we are visiting the in-laws) may be other ways that we save time.

Biases, Our Compass to Life

Biases are unconsciously developed by our brains to help us navigate through life. While those biases may be born and survive at the unconscious level, some are more implicit than others; some are more damaging than others. Let me offer an example with one of my "former" biases. While growing up in Spain, several of my friends and my brother were mugged on separate occasions. In most instances, my friends told me that the muggers were *gitanos* (gypsies). A large permanent community of gypsies had settled in an area around the Castle of Santa Barbara in Alicante, and since the mugging took place around that area, and my friends had told me their stories about being mugged, I jumped to the conclusion that all gypsies were either delinquent or beggars. This was an explicit bias. If I were walking alone at night and saw a group of gypsies, I would

---

22 Aubrey C. Daniels, *Bringing out the Best in People* (McGraw Hill, 2000); F.G. Ashby, B.O. Turner, and J.C. Horvitz, "Cortical and Basal Ganglia Contributions to Habit Learning and Automaticity," *Trends in Cognitive Sciences* 14 (5) (2010): 208–215, doi:10.1016/j.tics.2010.02.001.

make myself look as big as possible, and just in case, change routes to avoid running into them. I also avoided the area around the castle at nighttime (despite having one of the best places to eat *papas bravas*).

One day, I was sharing my views with my father, an entrepreneur with his own construction business, and he told me a story. While developing several large projects, he realized that their normal crews were being stretched too thin, and he told the supervisor to hire more people. For some reason, only a few candidates showed up, among them, two individuals of gypsy-background (I do not use the term *Roma* since I am not sure that the gypsies in my hometown were truly Roma people). The supervisor, my uncle, hired all of them.

On the first day of work, some tools went missing. On the second day, the two gypsy workers did not show up. On the third day, the two missing workers, led by their respective wives, showed up with the tools. My father happened to be on site, so the two ladies respectfully explained to him that "their husbands made a mistake and borrowed some tools for a home project without thinking about the potential implications. They missed work while working on said project the second day, and if they were allowed to work again, they (the wives) would make sure that it did not happen ever again and that the two gentlemen would become my father's best workers." My dad believes in second chances, so he agreed without much thought. He told me that over the last ten years, these two gentlemen had been his best workers—reliable, hard-working, thankful, and dedicated. They had even brought in other "relatives" over time and had now formed his most productive construction crew. That story changed my bias.

Indeed, biases stem from our need to classify things. As previously mentioned, our brain fights ambiguity by developing patterns and groupings. Most of those groupings are extremely helpful. For example, early on we establish that any container that holds liquid is a type of glass, despite the color of the container, or its height, width, or material. We may become more discriminating with time and learn to differentiate a juice glass from a wine glass from a whisky glass, but the functionality is clear —this type of container holds liquid from which we can comfortably (or not so comfortably) drink. We do not need to relearn what the functionality of a glass is every time we encounter one of a different color or shape.

The same could be said when we are drinking or eating any food or liquid that produces steam. Our brain lets us know, "Hey, that's hot!" We do not even need to read the *caution* warning on a McDonald's cup of coffee to know that it is hot. Ok, maybe some individuals do, but for the most part, when we observe steam, most of us will realize that it is hot and drink it carefully to avoid burning ourselves. Although it could be a glass full of liquid nitrogen, the steam is the liquid nitrogen becoming a gas, but that's not a very normal pattern to be exposed to unless you happen to work at a research lab.

Prehistorical Brain

When it comes to grouping people, our brain uses the same methodology with one caveat—our prehistoric brain will seek to classify the individual friend (one of ours) or foe (not one of ours). This is a concept that was first identified by sociologist William Sumner in 1906 as an explanation for the perception of existing conflict among different groups or tribes.[23] Why is this significant? Individuals from our in-groups (aka inter-group or tribe) pop up as *friends* for the most part. Most individuals in the out-group fall into the *foe* category.

---

23 Marilynn B. Brewer, "In-Group Bias in the Minimal Intergroup Situation: A Cognitive-Motivational Analysis," *Psychological Bulletin* 86, no. 2 (1979): 307.

Again, why is this relevant? Numerous studies tell us that this concept of in- and out-groups are at the root of most biases and prejudices. We start putting people into categories early on as we differentiate between caregivers and other individuals. And we develop new in- and out-groups regularly with incredible ease. In 1971, Tajfel and colleagues showed how by randomly assigning students to different groups (those that love the cubist and impressionist painter Klee versus those that prefer the abstract painter Kandinsky), their behaviors toward each other changed, supporting and benefiting those members from their in-group and discriminating and competing against those individuals in the out-group.[24] One single element, the personal preference of Kandinsky or Klee, was enough to like or dislike other individuals in the experiment. This exemplifies how easy it is to grab onto one specific perceived attribute (fictional in this case) to create a separate in-group and to come up with a supposed conflict with the other.

To be fair, not everyone agrees with this concept, which is known as tribalism. Ryan Cooper recently wrote an opinion piece in *The Week* magazine on the so-called political tribalism in the United States. He disagreed with the use of the term *tribalism*, arguing that, "*[T]ribes do not behave as moronically as described, and the problem with American politics has more to do with modernity than Americans reverting to some imagined atavistic state.*"[25] He proposes that when people engage in tribalism, they usually resorts to violence to resolve arguments and conflicts to silence the other group(s), a very colonist solution. The current conflict between the right and the left in the United States, Cooper argues, is just a modern

---

24 Henri Tajfel, Michael G. Billig, Robert P. Bundy, and Claude Flament, "Social Categorization and Intergroup Behaviour," *European Journal of Social Psychology* 1, no. 2 (1971): 149–178.

25 Ryan Cooper, "Tribalism Is Not the Problem," *The Week*, October 19, 2018, http://theweek.com/articles/802580/tribalism-not-problem.

societal conflict, centered on interpretations of laws, the role of the government, and modern norms governing this country. I am not going to split hairs with Mr. Cooper on the meaning of tribalism. I will support the academic definition of *tribe* and *tribalism*, which fits with the main narrative of this book and is accepted by most sociologists and psychologists.

And, by the way, our tribes are constantly changing. Every time a new generation enters the workplace, we face a new set of expectations, changing values, and evolving beliefs—a different tribe. This is extremely relevant nowadays. In the United States, the demographics over the next decade will change significantly.[26] According to the US Census Bureau, 33 percent of the adult population belongs to a racial or ethnic minority, but the percentage grows to 45 percent if we consider the child and adolescent populations.[27] That 46 percent will be the new wave joining the workforce. We will have to learn how to lead these new tribes.

These new tribes not only come with fresh ideas but also with a new way of working. They come with innovative ideas, many of them resulting in new ways of working. Organizations have (and are) spending billions of US dollars explaining to Gen Xers and baby boomers how to better work with and integrate the millennial generation. Now, Gen Z is starting to join the workplace. Imagine what will happen when those generations are also multicultural. What new challenges will we face? The simple answer is to improve your self-awareness, use critical thinking, and curb your biased decisions, and you will be ok.

---

26 William O'Hare, "The Changing Child Population of the United States: Analysis of Data from the 2010 Census," (working paper, The Annie E. Casey Foundation, Kids Count, November 2011).

27 US Census Bureau, *2010 Census Redistricting Data (Public Law 94–171), Summary File* (2010 Census of Population and Housing, Washington DC): Tables P1 and P2, https://www.census.gov/prod/cen2010/doc/pl94-171.pdf.

Adding to the complexity, tribalism is a situational phenomenon that varies with the environment and social surroundings. We
all project ourselves in different ways depending on our surroundings—at home with family, at work with coworkers, or at the pub with
friends, we project a different *I*, a different persona, a different presence, and a different personal brand that fits the situation. Still, the
foundation for those personas are built on the same set of values and
ideals, and we prioritize some over others to fit the situation. However,
all are still present.

The Social Animal

At the risk of sounding repetitive, allow me to write once more
that we are social animals. As such, we belong to a specific culture
with which we identify. Many definitions of culture refer to this phenomenon. Sociologist Geert Hofstede defined culture as "the collective programming of the mind that distinguishes the members of one
group or category of people from others."[28] Differentiating between
groups is an essential task of belonging to any culture or similar group
of individuals.

Organizations also develop a culture as well as a collection
of subcultures, such as the sales and marketing unit culture or the
engineering division culture. Our in-groups involve a set of different subgroups, and we adapt our behaviors to the subgroup with
whom we are interacting.[29] In the same way, this mental grouping of
individuals is evident in the manner that one chooses to behave in
the workplace.

---

28 Geert Hofstede, "Dimensionalizing Cultures: The Hofstede Model in Context," *Online
    Readings in Psychology and Culture* 2 (2011), https://doi.org/10.9707/2307-
    0919.1014.

29 Other factors that determine our behaviors include emotional state (negative or
    positive emotions); external pressures, such as deadlines; organizational culture,
    including power distance and uncertainty avoidance; personal life events;
    physiological state (hours slept, health…).

With an increasingly diverse workforce, we encounter daily scenarios that challenge our preconceived tribalism. Allow me to begin by pointing out my definition of diversity. By diversity, I include a plethora of factors such as race, religion, lifestyle, gender, sexual orientation, age, generational differences, political convictions, culture, disabilities, education, regional differences, rural versus urban, and many others.[30] We are not just limiting ourselves to the narrow legal definition of what diversity is. As leaders of an organization, we must acknowledge the necessity to expand our definition of diversity as much as possible to truly manage our biases in the workplace. Expanding the definition of diversity allows us to expand our self-awareness. For example, nowadays, one of the biggest biases that we face in the workforce relates to obesity. Studies have shown that we are most likely to promote, hire, and give pay raises to individuals in good physical condition while the opposite is also true[31].

The Center for Creative Leadership defines leadership as the social process that "enables individuals to work together as a cohesive group to produce collective results."[32] This definition implies that individuals must develop and use different relationships to accomplish a common goal, in a coordinated manner, using a set of limited and diverse resources in the most effective manner. Just as the success of the organization is partially dependent on the organizational culture, our success as leaders is determined by our ability to

---

30   Jamal AbuSneineh, Garlapati Ashok, Kelly A. Bernish, Dale Brito, Rixio E. Medina, Terrie S. Norris, and Linda G. Rhodes, "Adding Diversity Awareness to Our Leadership Skill Set" (conference paper, ASSE Professional Development Conference and Exhibition, American Society of Safety Engineers, 2008).

31   Hosoda, Megumi, Eugene F. Stone - Romero, and Gwen Coats. "The effects of physical attractiveness on job - related outcomes: A meta - analysis of experimental studies." Personnel psychology 56, no. 2 (2003): 431-462.

32   "Direction, Alignment, Commitment: Achieving Better Results through Leadership," webinar presented by Cindy McCauley and Lynn Fick-Cooper, Center for Creative Leadership, 2015.

recognize, acknowledge, and manage our personal biases in favor or against certain groups to optimize the organization's diversity.

"But, Juan, I have implemented mandatory diversity and inclusion training in my organization. Do I really need to read this book?" Yes, definitely. While a well-engineered and implemented diversity and inclusion research-based program with cultural intelligence development as one of the main goals may be effective, research shows that most mandatory diversity programs are (1) not increasing diversity, (2) have a tendency to activate bias, and/or, (3) could spark backlash within the organization.[33] Diversity programs that focus solely on unconscious bias training have the potential to make biases even worse by placing the blame on managers instead of looking at the overall organizational culture or other environmental elements.[34] Research conducted by Dobbin and Kalev and published in the *Harvard Business Review* found that most diversity programs focus on controlling managers' behaviors and have a lasting effect of one to two days...yes, *days*, not weeks, not months, but one to two days.

The point of most diversity programs is to reduce bias in decision-making, hiring processes, performance evaluation, and internal grievances. In their research, Dobbin and Kalev found that current diversity programs are not effective in alleviating bias in any of those areas. On the other hand, programs focused on voluntary training (versus mandatory trainings), mentoring programs, engaging managers in working for diversity and increasing managers' contact with women and minorities, did have a positive effect on diversity and reduced overall bias.[35] Making managers better leaders through

---

33 Frank Dobbin and Alexandra Kalev, "Why Diversity Programs Fail," *Harvard Business Review* 94, no. 7 (2016): 14.

34 David Rock and Heidi Grant, "Is Your Company's Diversity Training Making You More Biased?" *Strategy+Business*, May 8, 2017, Issue 88, https://www.strategy-business.com/blog/Is-Your-Companys-Diversity-Training-Making-You-More-Biased.

35 Dobbin and Kalev, "Why Diversity Programs Fail," 2016, 9.

self-awareness, social accountability, exposure to other groups, and improvements in executive presence are more effective strategies in combating bias and improving diversity.

Discovering Our Biases

As I already mentioned at the beginning of this chapter, we all have biases. Some of these biases are based on implicit associations or subconscious pairing. How early are these biases ingrained in our psyche? Recently, a study in the United Kingdom, involving over one thousand children, ages four through eight, showed that most children had already made up their minds about what jobs were gender-specific.[36] For example, 40 percent of the children believed that doctors should be men, and 44 percent thought engineers need to be men. Another study found that gender bias played a role in many organizations' hiring practices, with certain jobs subconsciously paired to certain genders.[37] Biases are learned early on and affect every decision we make throughout our lives.

---

36   Robert Knight, "Many Schoolchildren Don't Think Women Can Be Builders, Footballers, or Lorry Drivers, Survey Finds," March 12, 2018, video on *Independent*, https://www.independent.co.uk/news/media/tv-radio/school-children-jobs-men-women-tv-show-cbeebies-bitz-and-bob-cbeebies-a8250906.html.

37   Carol Isaac, Barbara Lee, and Molly Carnes, "Interventions That Affect Gender Bias in Hiring: a Systematic Review," *Academic Medicine: Journal of the Association of American Medical Colleges* 84, no. 10 (2009): 1440.

THE NATURE OF PREJUDICE

The Way Our Brains Are Wired

No book on prejudice and bias should exist without a reference to Gordon Allport´s *The Nature of Prejudice*.[38] As we have established, leaders operate in a society, so they are susceptible to societal biases and prejudices. Prejudice is fundamentally the way we think or feel about an individual or group. Discrimination refers to the actions we take based on that negative prejudice. While I did promise that I would avoid making this book into an academic treatise, it is important to review Allport's book because it sets one of the first foundation on bias, a type of prejudice. Using a social scientific approach, Allport introduced one of the most comprehensive research-based compilations on prejudice in 1954. Reading the original preface, one can only question how much humans have evolved over the last six decades since the book was first published – the social issues faced by some groups when the first edition was published, are similar to the social issues faced by present-day minorities.

By definition, prejudice is an unjustified fictional positive or negative attitude toward another person based on in-group or tribal membership. Bias is a type of prejudice for or against another human being or concept that we often consider unfair.[39] Writing, "While some of this endless antagonism seems based upon a realistic conflict of interest, most of it, we suspect, is a product of the fears of the

---

38 Gordon W. Allport, *The Nature of Prejudice Unabridged, Twenty-Fifth Anniversary Edition* (New York: Perseus Books Publishing, LLC, 1979).

39 Ian Sawyer, "What is the Difference Between Prejudice and Bias," Quora answer, April 22, 2016, https://www.quora.com/What-is-the-difference-between-prejudice-and-bias.

imagination,"[40] Allport captured the general psychological undertones of prejudice. Biases in the workplace are based on fears and preconceived ideas that we as leaders need to challenge.

Most prejudices originate from a story we have created to explain what we do not know. As someone once told me, "The cure for boredom is curiosity, and there's no cure for curiosity." Asking questions and being curious is the best antidote against prejudice. Prejudice is borne from assumptions, in most instances, fictional limitations and bridges in understanding that we create to explain an event or people. Ignorance about a culture, lack of curiosity or imagination, and laziness are the main sources of prejudice.

Allport wrote *The Nature of Prejudice* a decade after the end of World War II. During this time of economic prosperity, against the backdrop of the Korean War stalemate, the United States was still feeling the effects of absorbing the newly arrived immigrant masses of WWII. It was also struggling to understand the global repercussions of the newly established nation of Israel and the infant stages of the globalized economy borne out of the Marshall Plan. The country, led by president Eisenhower and a Republican-controlled Congress, struggled with societal biases and integration of the newly settled European immigrants (mostly Irish and Catholic), the growing Jewish population, and the existing African-American population. Change the nationalities, Irish or Italians for Mexican or Central Americans, Catholics for Muslims, and update other era-based details such low-end manufacturing jobs for low-skilled jobs, and one can find many parallels between the mid-fifties and today. Allport´s book presented a provocative and research-supported interpretation of prejudice, the bases for prejudices, and an array of potential solutions.

---

40   Allport, *The Nature of Prejudice Unabridged*, xv.

To understand this book, we need first to understand some of the concepts Allport presented. Early in the book, Allport defended his preference for the term *ethnicity* instead of *race*. Ethnicity, he argued, encompassed a larger portion of the population affected by prejudice. Allport defined ethnicity by the characteristics of a group of individuals with similar physical traits, national and/or regional culture, common language, religion, or perceived social or ideological identities. Allport acknowledged that *ethnicity* fell short of encompassing all potential victims of societal prejudices. For example, the term did not include gender-, caste-, occupation-, economic status-, or politically-motivated prejudices. But *ethnicity* included more victim groups of societal prejudice than *race* did.

Allport also differentiated between *prejudice* and *discrimination*, arguing that "prejudice is ultimately a problem of personality formation and development; no two cases of prejudice are precisely the same,"[41] an argument supported throughout this book. On the other hand, Allport defined discrimination as denying "individuals or groups of people equality of treatment which they may wish"[42]. Why are these two terms different? One could hold a certain prejudice and actively avoid letting that prejudice influence one's decisions, for example, during hiring or promotion procedures.

Sources of Societal Prejudice

The book includes a series of potential sources of societal prejudice. Many still apply in present time—fear of immigration; religious ignorance and intolerance; denigration of certain groups; overgeneralization and stereotyping of groups; misogynist societal and political systems. In general, I would argue, that the contemporary term of

---

41   Allport, *The Nature of Prejudice Unabridged*, 41.
42   Allport, *The Nature of Prejudice Unabridged*, 51.

cultural intelligence could partially encompass Allport's references to *open-mindedness* (or lack thereof), *socio-cultural* knowledge, and *situational* flexibility. As we saw before, cultural intelligence, a term that goes beyond the notion of cultural sensitivity and self-awareness, refers to the ability to relate to and interact effectively with an open mind in culturally diverse situations to accomplish business goals.

Allport introduced many of the concepts we have talked about throughout this book. For example, in parts II and III of his book, Allport introduced and analyzed several psychological factors that feed an individual's level of prejudice, such as cognitive dissonance; in- versus out-group perspectives; the effects of individual personality; social- and cultural-upbringing; familiarity; anchoring, or referencing; and categorization. His in-depth presentation of different types of prejudices, as well as the dynamics of prejudice, provides a window into the human mind, outlining the foundation to understand, address, and reduce individual prejudicial behaviors. In the following pages, I will discuss many of the concepts introduced by Allport in his book, to the arena of law enforcement.

An Extension of Institutional Bias

The concept of unconscious biases and prejudices is not a new one. Tversky and Kahneman (1974) studied the practical reliance of humans on a limited number of heuristic or common-sense rules that help simplify judgmental operations. Humans rely on certain anchors to quickly and efficiently evaluate a situation and act accordingly. Numerous studies refer to the effect of implicit social bias and institutional prejudice on individual decisions. Institutional prejudice involves stereotyping and discriminatory practices within the organization's culture that perpetuates the biased treatment of certain individuals within and outside the organization. Some of those institutional biases reflect implicit social biases. Kirsten Weir defined implicit biases as "attitudes or stereotypes that can influence [our] beliefs, actions, and decisions, even though [we´re] not consciously aware of them and [don´t] express those beliefs verbally to [ourselves] or others."[43]

Implicit biases are built within our cognitive processes, our interpretation of the world around us. Social cognition researchers and social psychologists agree on the existence of two different cognitive processing systems: a) the type 1 (also, known as the intuitive system) cognitive process and b) the type 2 (also known as the reflective system) cognitive system.[44] In his book *The Righteous Mind*, Jon Haidt visualizes the mind as a rider on an elephant. The rider´s job is to serve and control the elephant. Type 1 is the elephant, powerful, intuitive, synergetic, large, and difficult to control; Type 2 is the rider, small, logical, and calculating, but lazy and with limited influence on the elephant.

The intuitive cognitive system (type 1) is more effortless and operates at an unconscious level. It operates on the knowledge and memories from past experiences, cemented by a personal system of values and norms. Most of what happens within that system stays outside the conscious awareness.

This system regulates what individuals refer to as intuition or "gut feeling."[45] It takes the limited information available, fills in the

43 Kirsten Weir, "Policing in Black and White," *Monitor on Psychology* 47, no. 11 (2016): 36–43.

44 Jon Haidt, *The Righteous Mind: Why Good People Are Divided by Politics and Religion* (New York: Vintage, 2013).
    Daniel Kahneman, *Thinking, Fast and Slow* (New York: Farrar, Straus, and Giroux, 2011).
    Daniel Kahneman, Dan Lovallo, and Olivier Sibony, "Before We Make That Big Decision," *Harvard Business Review* 89, no. 6 (2011): 50–60; Amos Tversky and Daniel Kahneman, "Judgment under Uncertainty: Heuristics and Biases," *Science* 185, no. 4157 (1974): 1124–1131.

45 Rick Trinkner and Phillip Atiba Goff, "The Color of Safety: the Psychology of Race and Policing," *The SAGE Handbook of Global Policing* (2016): 61–81.

gaps of knowledge with familiar information based on the context familiar information and concludes in a narrative regarding what the truth is and what actions to take—all in a split second. Stereotypes and generalizations support this thinking process and vice versa, forming a looping system- my thinking process is partially dependent on the stereotypes and generalizations which are also reinforced by the unconscious filtering of information that supports my stereotypes and generalizations, reinforcing my thinking process and so on.

Type 1 behaviors could be developed through repetition and experiential learning. Some examples of this behaviors could be easy mathematical calculations such as 2+2, or knowing the distance to an object based on the size. Driving a car between two familiar points (i.e. work and home, grocery store and home) can also become a Type 1 behavior through repetition and experience.

The reflective system (Type 2) involves an individual´s ability to deliberately pursue rational, logical, and mathematical computations. It is home to one´s critical thinking. The reflective system is slow but deliberate and intentional.[46] It involves conscious, rational thinking and requires concentration and focus, using up most of one´s cognitive resources and limiting other simultaneous activities. Activities that involve Type 2 thinking are more tiresome; they consume more cognitive energy and engage more individual resources. Driving in adverse weather conditions or through an unknown route would require as to engage our reflective system. Seeking for a specific person in social setting or engaging in quantum physics would require a more deliberate cognitive attitude.

As mentioned, the intuitive cognitive process involves the use of mental shortcuts. Mental shortcuts are essential to an individual´s healthy psychological wellbeing by linking pieces of information to

---

46 Kahneman, Thinking, Fast and Slow.

memories for quick memory retrieval.[47] This process also develops shortcuts to encode memories, which link events to existing stereotypes. For example, when someone hears that an individual overdosed on crack, the assumption might be that the victim belonged to a minority group. When the drug is opioids, the first assumption might be that the individual was white; some individuals may even pinpoint rural post-industrialized America. These assumptions may be partially supported by statistics, an in-group belief, or reinforced by the media.

This memory recall process results from the brain's development of certain patterns or schemas during the encoding of new information, potentially affecting the factuality of the memory itself.[48] Studies point out that during ambiguous and uncertain situations, implicit biases could influence one's judgments and behaviors through unconscious assumptions and heuristics.[49] We believe, for example, that more people die from car crashes than heart attacks because the news reports more deaths from car accidents than deaths from heart attacks. You have a one in five chance of dying from a heart attack over a lifetime, compared to one in eighty-four chances of dying in a car accident.[50] This reasoning process is known as *disambiguation*. Based on incomplete information, we create our own logic and story to explain our conclusions. Type 1 system excels at constructing the best possible stories based on an individual's

47 Kahneman, *Thinking, Fast and Slow*; Tversky and Kahneman, "Judgment under Uncertainty: Heuristics and Biases," 1124–1131.

48 Justin D. Levinson, "Forgotten Racial Equality: Implicit Bias, Decision Making, and Misremembering," *Duke LJ* 57 (2007): 345.

49 Katherine B. Spencer, Amanda K. Charbonneau, and Jack Glaser, "Implicit Bias and Policing," *Social and Personality Psychology Compass* 10, no. 1 (2016): 50–63.

50 "International Shark Attack File, Risk of Death," Florida Museum of Natural History, updated February 1, 2018, https://www.floridamuseum.ufl.edu/shark-attacks/odds/compare-risk/death/.

limited experiences and factual knowledge, filling any gaps in information with more intuitive information.[51]

In one study, college students and police officers were subliminally exposed to black faces, white faces or not faces at all. Then, the students and the police officers were shown different objects. Those individuals that were exposed to black faces, were better able to identify crime-related objects.[52] The research subjects also paid more attention to black faces when introduced to the concept of crime.

Our attitudes and behaviors are affected by the exposure to elements in our environment, at the conscious or unconscious level. Associative priming can undermine our own free will[53]. In a classic study conducted by J.A Bargh in 1996, students were asked to solve a linguistic scrambled-sentence puzzle, without realizing that some students had more "elderly" related words (elderly, Florida, lone, grey...) in their puzzle. Subsequently, the students were asked to walk to a different part of the university, and they were timed. Those students that resolved the linguistic puzzles heavy on elderly wording walked slower than the other students[54].

The relationship between associative priming and environmental exposure to cultural elements, such as the belief that more people die in car accidents than from heart attack because of news reports could impact the level of cultural biases injected into any

51   Haidt, The Righteous Mind: Why Good People Are Divided by Politics and Religion.

52   Jennifer L. Eberhardt, Phillip Atiba Goff, Valerie J. Purdie, and Paul G. Davies, "Seeing Black: Race, Crime, and Visual Processing," Journal of Personality and Social Psychology 87, no. 6 (2004): 876.

53   Di Nucci, Ezio. "Priming effects and free will." International Journal of Philosophical Studies 20, no. 5 (2012): 725-734.

54   Bargh, John A., Mark Chen, and Lara Burrows. "Automaticity of social behavior: Direct effects of trait construct and stereotype activation on action." Journal of personality and social psychology 71, no. 2 (1996): 230.

individual's implicit biases.[55] Because of stereotypes developed in movies, television, or other forms of social entertainment, we may come to believe that certain behaviors are connected to those stereotypes. For example, cartoons used to picture French people carrying a baguette under their arms, wearing black berets, sporting funny moustaches, and acting extremely romantic. If you ask someone what nationality is the most romantic, most people would immediately think of the French. The concept of *romantic* would prime or predispose most people to associate it with French people, a cultural bias created by the entertainment industry.

Associative priming has consequences beyond cartoons and the romanticism of the French people. In a study that analyzed the co-occurrence of certain terms with the words *black* and *white*, researchers detected a strong correlation between the use of *black* with words such as *poor*, *violent*, *lazy*, and *dangerous*. Words that co-occurred with *white* were *wealthy*, *progressive*, *conventional*, *successful*, and *educated*.[56] These studies support the concept that exposure to cultural representations such as newspapers and other media imply exposure to the implicit racial prejudices upheld by the existing institutional racism.

Regardless of the culture of origin, a culture specific bias and prejudice will taint the way we perceive the world and, therefore, the way we make decisions. For example, coming from Spain, I may understand the cultural significance behind bullfights but believe that eating dog is barbaric. Still, I would have no issue eating a steak

---

55   Paul Verhaeghen, Shelley N. Aikman, and Ana E. Van Gulick, "Prime and Prejudice: Co-occurrence in the Culture as a Source of Automatic Stereotype Priming," *British Journal of Social Psychology* 50, no. 3 (2011): 501–518; David R. Williams, "How Racism Makes Us Sick," November 2016, a *TEDMED talk*, www.ted.com/talks/david_r_williams_how_racism_makes_us_sick#t-630945.

56   Verhaeghen, Aikman, and Van Gulick, "Prime and Prejudice: Co-occurrence in the Culture as a Source of Automatic Stereotype Priming," 501–518.

while a Hindu will view killing a sacred cow. Someone from a Buddhist background may perceive killing any type of animal as cruel.

The fascinating thing is that we may not even notice that this is happening for many reasons. The people in our intra-groups, or tribes, will most likely not question our biased decisions. "Why wouldn't you want to eat a nice juicy steak?" After all, the members of our tribes would use the same heuristics to analyze the information and make a decision, which would mostly certainly be similar to our own.

"There is nothing wrong with eating beef; it's a good source of protein." At a macro-context level, our own biases would be reinforced by the institutionalized bias in the news, politics, business, and economic practices. "The beef industry lobbyists will reinforce the benefits of eating beef as the perfect source of protein. After all, television reports now tell us that."

Now, let's move away from a specific country or geographical circle and into our own organizational culture and practices that govern it. What happens if we surround ourselves with executives who share our beliefs? Have we hired employees from the same handful of institutions or from within our industry? How much diversity (gender, age, race, social, and economic background) do we have in our top executive team? Our R&D group? Our Marketing and Sales group? Does our foreign subsidiary in X country have a fair representation of X-citizens in the company's management, and does that representation match the diverse composition of X country, or is it favoring a specific group within that country?

What about business decisions? When a business decision is made, who is part of that decision? Do we have anyone playing the role of devil's advocate, or following the Tenth Man rule?[57] The Tenth

---

57   Yosef Kuperwasser, "Lessons from Israel's Intelligence Reforms," (analysis paper, number 14, The Saban Center for Middle East Policy at the Brookings Institution, October 2007), www.brookings.edu. https://www.brookings.edu/wp-content/uploads/2016/06/10_intelligence_kuperwasser.pdf.

Man rule argues that when a team or group of individuals decide unanimously to take certain action (exploiting a new opportunity or resolving a problem), at least one individual has to prepare as if the new opportunity will fail or the problem will not be resolved. Originally, this concept was developed by the Israeli Intelligence forces in the aftermath of the Yom Kippur War (1973) to prepare for the least-evident possibility of failure.

It is also worth questioning the assumptions or guidelines within our managerial decision processes, as well as the corporate traditions that overshadow our business practices. For example, think about that five-day executive retreat in Scottsdale, Arizona, to enjoy a bit of golfing in the downtime. What are the assumptions we are making with that simple act? When you think about golf players, what are the assumptions you make about those individuals? Who would enjoy playing golf? Think about age, gender, race. We should ask ourselves those questions, and then we will be engaged in critical thinking, the first step to reducing the effects of implicit bias in our judgment and decision-making processes.

SOCIAL IDENTITY AND SELF-AWARENESS

How Do We Fit within the Dominant Culture?

Humans are complex entities. In his autobiography, Kahneman wrote about this complexity. To illuminate this, the Nobel Prize winner narrated one of his experiences in occupied Paris in late 1941 or early 1942 as an immigrant Lithuanian Jew.[58] One night when he was a child, he was heading home after curfew, wearing his yellow-star-marked sweater inside out. A German officer, wearing a black SS uniform, asked him to approach and proceeded to hug him with tears in his eyes. The officer showed him a picture of young boy and gave him some money before letting him go. Most likely, the young Kahneman reminded him of his child back at home. That encounter could have gone many ways, but the German SS officer looked at the situation through the eyes of a sad, homesick father missing his family, and not through the eyes of an SS officer. We are complex animals, governed by a prehistorically engineered cognitive processor, our brains.

Before we continue, let me restate an important point. Based on the findings of most of the research I've read , I would like to throw my agreement behind Allport´s hypothesis that humans are not born biased but that biases are learned.[59] While I would agree that who we are is a combination of nature and nurture, since there is not much that we can do with our nature-side, other than genetic modifications

---

58 Daniel Kahneman and Smith Vernon, "Daniel Kahneman: Biographical," *The Nobel Prize* (website), accessed September 1, 2018, https://www.nobelprize.org/prizes/economics/2002/kahneman/auto-biography/.

59 Allport, *The Nature of Prejudice Unabridged*.

or medication, we are going to focus on the nurture-side in this book, the part that we can actually control.

An internal moral consciousness compass guides the behaviors, actions, and thoughts of most humans. That moral compass is calibrated by a set of internalized values derived from our interactions with specific groups in our society. We adhere to certain societal values (to higher and lower degrees) unconsciously, without much analysis of the societal rules by which we abide.[60] Those societal rules contain some biases as well, invisible to our consciousness and disguised as traditions, ways of living, values, and mores. Unfortunately, sometimes those traditions and societal rules are born from ignorance or lack of exposure.

In 1969, researchers Knowles and Shah conducted a study on the effect that cultural bias had in children in three different locations—an urban Detroit area, a suburban Detroit area, and India.[61] The study found that the differences in interpretations of different scenarios between the inner-city Detroit children and suburban Detroit children were as marked as the differences in interpretations between the US children and the children from India. This study concluded that, even within one single country (United States) and city (Detroit), the cultural bias of two groups could be as pronounced as the gap between two completely different national cultures (the United States and India).

Culture plays a central role in developing those social biases. In this context, I believe that the definition of culture by the renowned Dutch sociologist Geert Hofstede would be the most applicable. Hofstede defined culture as "the collective programming of the mind

---

60 Dan Ariely, *The (Honest) Truth about Dishonesty: How We Lie to Everyone—Especially Ourselves* (New York: Harper Perennial, 2012).

61 Richard T. Knowles and Gunvant B. Shah, "Cultural Bias in Testing: An Exploration," *The Journal of Social Psychology* 77, no. 2 (1969): 285–286.

that distinguishes members of one group from others."[62] His definition implies the concepts of social ties (collective programming) as well the differentiating element implied in culture.

An example of culture is the corporate or organizational culture within which we, as executives, regularly operate. An organizational culture also involves patterns of shared values, norms, ethics, and beliefs just as you would find in any other type of social culture. Organizational culture governs employees' actions and behaviors and is supported by processes, rules, and guidelines. As we stated before, that organizational culture could determine the factors influencing some of a leader's biases and prejudices. Because we need to conform to the beliefs of our in-group, stereotypes are instilled at an early age as a social survival reflex. By *early age*, I am referring to actual age in years (childhood) but also to the recent college graduate joining a firm and trying to make her mark. That cultural knowledge and experience set rules on how societal members think, feel, and perceive reality.[63]

Before we move forward to solutions for improving our self-awareness as leaders, it important to introduce the concepts of dominant culture and subculture.[64] We are not affected by one sole culture or one single set of in-group rules. In any given day, we adjust to the rules of our environment. Different behaviors emerge based on the rules and norms governing the culture or subculture of that scenario.

In the previous scenarios, a dominant culture sets the rules, rewards system, and the norms for behavior within a society. Those

---

62 Geert Hofstede, "Dimensionalizing Cultures: the Hofstede Model in Context," *Online Readings in Psychology and Culture* 2, no. 1 (2011): 8, https://doi.org/10.9707/2307-0919.1014.

63 Justin D. Levinson, "Forgotten Racial Equality: Implicit Bias, Decision-Making, and Misremembering," *Duke LJ* 57 (2007): 345.

64 Joel Lieske, "Can American Democracy Be Sustained? Immigration, Diversity, and Conflict" (conference paper, Midwestern Political Science Association, 1, 2007).

individuals who do not abide by these norms might form subcultures and subgroups within that dominant culture.[65] In some instances, those subcultures could be involuntary[66] because the dominant culture vilifies the groups' behaviors, pushing them to become an out-group. The marginalized group subsequently creates a comfort zone—a subculture.

While I partially agree with those researchers who argue that we are born with certain temperaments or personalities, I say that we are simply born with a predisposition toward certain personality traits, fed by physiological differences in certain hormonal levels, brain wiring, and pre-birth conditions. Those innate personality traits result in certain behaviors and prejudices when triggered by upbringing, exposure to in-group thinking, experiences, and culture. That governing culture and experiences shapes our personality. Once we have established those values in our formative years, any changes to that framework requires a reframing of those values.[67] Exposure to other groups or a dramatic event could cause this reframing.

Our culture is molded by the national, regional, or local culture to which we were exposed in our childhoods. In his book *Undoing Privilege*, Pease described the concept of hegemonic, or dominant culture, within a national culture as a socially constructed beliefs foundation that originate from a combination of historically developed psychological and sociological insights.[68] For example, the US's dominant culture is defined by ideologies borne from Euro-white

65   M. J. Moran (May 1997), "Intracultural Differences: a Differentiation Culture Study" (*Dissertation Abstracts International*), Section A, 57, 4822.

66   K. P. Gonzalez, "Campus Culture and the Experiences of Chicano Students in Predominantly White Colleges and Universities" (ASHE Annual Meeting Paper, 1999).

67   Nancy S. Isaacson and Sandra M. Wilson, "Secondary School Subcultures and the Implementation of Nontraditional School Schedules" (paper presented at the Annual Meeting of American Educational Research Association, New York, NY, April 8–12, 1996).

68   Bob Pease, *Undoing Privilege: Unearned Advantage in a Divided World* (Zed Books Ltd., 2013).

supremacy, patriarchal (or male-centered) society, Judeo-Christian, and heterosexual principles.[69] According to Morris and Peng, the dominant social tendency toward individualism in American culture originated from the Judeo-Christian notion of the individual soul and the English legal tradition of free will. [70]

On the topic of African American identity in the corporate world, my former colleague at the Center for Creative Leadership, Ancella Livers, suggested four steps to expand our understanding of identity.[71] In her book *Leading in Black and White*, she argues that an individual should (1) expand his ideas about identity, (2) determine the meaning of identity for him, (3) define how his identity is expressed, and (4) evaluate others' perceptions of those cultural-based behaviors.

Livers defined identity as "a dynamic interaction between how others perceive us and how we conceive of ourselves. It is influenced by many factors, such as race, gender, generational age, economic class, education, geographical location, and personal and collective history."[72]

To become better leaders, we need to not only know ourselves better but also understand and manage the perceptions of those around us. We need to be able to visualize our own social identity. Social identity is the part of an individual's self-concept and identification, regulated by the norms governing the different social groups that she psychologically belongs to at a cognitive level.[73] Social identity determines how (1) we categorize people into our in-groups

---

69 Pease, *Undoing Privilege: Unearned Advantage in a Divided World*.

70 Henri Tajfel, ed., *Social Identity and Intergroup Relations* (Cambridge University Press, 2010).

71 Ancella B. Livers and Keith A. Caver, *Leading in Black and White: Working across the Racial Divide in Corporate America* (California: Jossey-Bass, 2003).

72 Livers and Caver, *Leading in Black and White*, 28.

73 Livers and Caver, *Leading in Black and White*, 28.

or out-groups (and, by the way, our default mode is to categorize individuals as out-groups) based on shared beliefs, past experiences, specific visual or perceived characteristics, such gender, skin color, body shape, language, attitude, etc.; (2) how we identify ourselves with certain groups based on a sense of belonging, such as practicing the same religion, being of the same nationality in a foreign country, using the correct public restroom; and (3) we compare the in-group from the out-groups, most likely emphasizing our in-group´s superiority over the out-group.[74]

Language could also determine who is in our in-group, our tribe, and who is not.[75] Language helps us express thoughts, but would those thoughts even occur if we did not have a word for that particular emotion, event, object...? Let me be more specific. The Chinese language (and by the way, Latin as well), does not have a word for *yes* or *no*. In Chinese, one forms a negative by conjugating the verb in a negative manner (*bu* or *mei*, for example). Most Western languages have a clear word for yes and no. Who do you think will come across as the ruder group? Who do you think will come across as indecisive? What do you think will happen when a negotiation occurs between a very direct Dutch businesswoman and a not-so direct Chinese businessman? Does language create an obstacle to communication? Is it implying a perceived assumption about the other person? An even easier use of language that automatically assigns individuals to one group or another is gender specific nouns. In German and Spanish, words are divided into masculine, feminine, and in German, neutral genders. Just by speaking and thinking, we could be creating in- and out-groups.

---

74   Henri Tajfel and John C. Turner, "An Integrative Theory of Intergroup Conflict" in *The Social Psychology of Intergroup Relations* (California: Brooks/Cole Publishing, 1979).

75   Neel Burton, "How the Language You Speak Influences the Way You Think," *Psychology Today*, August 8, 2018, https://www.psychologytoday.com/us/blog/hide-and-seek/201808/how-the-language-you-speak-influences-the-way-you-think?amp.

One important aspect of in-groups and out-groups and a relevant differentiator for this conversation is that while we believe that certain differences exist between tribes, research shows that those differences are usually based on arbitrary assumptions and are not always true or necessarily beneficial to the group's identity. They may even be compatible with the preferences of other groups. Those differences are used, most of the time, to identify differences with people belonging to other groups, but they are not necessary to our own social identity.[76]

People want to align themselves with members of groups they believe share their identities and values, but because values and beliefs are abstract, we rely on behaviors, actions, and traditions that indicate those norms. Hans Rosling, in his book *Factfullness—Ten Reasons We're Wrong about the World and Why Things Are Better Than We Think*, asserted that we tend to polarize our views of the world.[77] We develop fallacies to classify things into opposite groups. Those fallacies and resulting misguided efforts to divide the world into opposite sides, inform our actions, and form part of our decision-making process.

A classic example of this is our view of the world. Have you ever looked at a European, African, or Asian view of the world? Most of us would use the map of the world, showing the United States on one side, Russia and China on the opposite side, and Europe in the middle. In Australia, the world map looks different. Oceania is in the middle. When I lived in China, I was confused when I saw the world map with China right in the middle. By the way, China in Mandarin Chinese is *ZhongGuo*, meaning middle or central kingdom.

_____

76 Taifel and Turner, "An Integrative Theory of Intergroup Conflict," 38.

77 Hans Rosling, Anna Rosling Rönnlund, and Ola Rosling, *Factfulness: Ten Reasons We're Wrong about the World—and Why Things are Better Than We Think* (Flatiron Books, 2018).

Nevertheless, we should not assume that our perspectives are the only valid perspectives. Remember that living in a VUCA world implies that there is more than one right answer to any dilemma. Therefore, there are many perspectives needed to look at the same challenge. For example, many groups share some of the same norms and values at their core, but believe to have the only valid and right perspective. For example, many individuals attribute the Golden rule—treat others as you would want to be treated—to the birth of Christianity. But references to the Golden Rule can be found in the writings of the Chinese philosopher Confucius, who lived in about 500 BC. Other references can be found in the Talmud, the central text of Rabbinic Judaism.

In order to understand most topics, we need to start my understanding who we are. Our perspective will be tainted by our social identity and self-awareness. Hence, to separate our social perception of any issue, we should delve on the underlying values and beliefs of our social identity, identifying potential assumptions that we may be making. I personally like to ask myself "how do I know that this is true?", "what is this so important to me?" and "what are the underlying risks of changing my perspective?".

Before we move forward, it's important that you develop a clear understanding of your own social identity. This is part of self-awareness for any leader and a requirement for understanding why certain things trigger us (think values), but it will also help you understand how you, as a human being first, leader second, come across to the people you interact with. For example, I am a somewhat big person. Currently (even though I seem to be shrinking every year), I am about 187 cm tall (6´1´´ for the metric-system-impaired reader) and weigh about 120 kg (around 270 pounds). I have a grayish beard, not much hair left (on my head) and still enjoy powerlifting

and rowing regularly. Why am I telling you this? During a family dinner at home, it was brought to my attention that I come across as a
scary guy to my daughters' friends. I had no idea, so I asked more
questions. It seemed that the fact that I only speak Spanish to my
daughters was one issue ("What is he saying?"), I don't do small talk
with their friends and I keep to myself ("Is he upset?" "Is he always
that grouchy?"), and I speak loudly ("Oh, definitely, upset and now,
yelling."). After finding out that I seemed to intimidate my daughters'
friends, I decided to speak in English when their friends were around
and also smile more, without looking too creepy (a very difficult balance that I achieved with my daughters' help).

One of my daughters' friend recently asked me to be one of
her references for her first job, and others are regulars at our family
dinners. It is important to understand how your social identity affects
other individuals. So, let's keep going.

Understanding Your Social Identity

To be more effective and unbiased leaders, we need to understand what our own identity represents. Understanding our own identities is essential for relationship management. In building corporate
relationships, trust and respect are fundamental. Stephanie Ruhle, an
MSNBC anchor, once stated in a conversation with NBC Late Night
Show host Seth Meyers that people build trust on relationships and
not information. Identity is about reciprocal relationships and how
others perceive us.

Former Center for Creative Leadership colleague and current
president of Aligned Impact LLC, Kelly Hannum, explained in her
book *Social Identity: Knowing Ourselves, Leading Others* visualized
social identity as "our way of thinking about ourselves and others

based on social groupings."[78] That social identity is composed of three sets of components that sometimes overlap. Those components are grouped under (1) the given identity defined by those attributes or conditions that we have no choice over, (2) the chosen identity characterized by those attributes that we have chosen, and (3) the core identity distinguished by those attributes that we believe make us unique as an individual.[79]

Let's move now from the theoretical to the practical mode of social identity and learn how to visualize our identity map.[80] Our identity map will provide us with a visual representation of our social identity based on the three components above.

First, grab a large blank piece of paper and a pen or pencil. Second, in the middle of the page, make a circle about five to ten centimeters (two to four inches) in diameter. That circle will represent the core traits and behaviors that we believe make us unique. For example, while you do not need to have taken previously these assessment, if you have recently completed a personality assessment (Workplace Big5, Myer-Briggs Type indicator, Hogan Personality Assessment, FIRO, Keirsey Assessment, DiSC), look at the personality traits that may define you at your core—introvert or extrovert, creative or implementer, organized, risk-taker or risk-avoider, reliable, fun, disciplined... Those characteristics define your autopilot, the most energy-efficient manner for us to behave—the path to happiness. Basically, these are the personality characteristics that will kick on when you are tired, stressed, or under distress. For example, I am an introvert with a handful of good friends; I am not afraid of taking risks in certain areas of my life, but I play it conservative in others; I have a tendency to use my organizational skills to break down complexity

---

78   Kelly Hannum, *Social Identity: Knowing Yourself, Leading Others* (Pfeiffer, 2007).

79   Hannum, *Social Identity: Knowing Yourself, Leading Others*, 12.

80   Hannum, *Social Identity: Knowing Yourself, Leading Others*, 14.

and compensate for my horrible memory retention; I am a reliable individual; and I am a direct and frank communicator. What is at your core? Think about it and write down those words that define you and contribute to your uniqueness.

Ok, we have now completed the traits and behaviors that make us unique. The second step is our chosen identity. Draw a larger circle around the centered core circle. In this circle (we still have one more circle to draw), we will write the words (use one single word when possible for each chosen aspect) that define the aspects of our life we have chosen for ourselves. For example, it could be our position in the company (manager, director, engineer, janitor, CEO, financial officer); it could be the type of work we do (professor, teacher, researcher, accountant, carpenter, electrician); it could be our hobby (powerlifter, motorcyclist, jogger, volunteer, bible student); or it could be related to our education, our career, our geographical identity (we may identify ourselves not with the place where we were born but with a different location for a different reason), our sports, political, or religious affiliation—any aspect of our life that we have chosen to identify with.

Finally, draw one final circle around the other two circles. This will cover those aspects of our identity that have been given to us. These are things we may not have chosen or may not even necessarily identify with. For example, our race, gender, nationality, age, physical characteristics, overall health, our relation to other individuals (father, son, husband, uncle, or cousin), even our religion could be a given. We may have been born within a family, social group, country, religion, or geographical area where the intricacies of that society do not allow choice without serious and/or unwanted repercussions. Or we may have been born in a specific region of a country that we identify with more than the actual country or attached nationality.

Or what about the individual who does not look their age? We all know individuals who do not look their age and/or do not act like the stereotypical person in that age range. By the way, ageism seems to be one of the latest and more acceptable stereotypes – why does the concept and expectations of age differ between gender? Why is it ok to refer to someone as "old"? For example, I just heard a debate on the radio about how Joe Biden and Bernie Sanders are "too old" to be the democratic candidates for the US presidential elections of 2020. Why is that ok to say? Sorry, going off topic… let's continue with our identity map.

Now we have developed our identity map. But how is that relevant to our biases and prejudice? Think back to the conversation about in- and out-groups. What we have now identified is a long list of potential in-groups with their respective out-groups. Remember that we like to put people, groups, and other things into opposing groups? We work better when we polarize ideas and concepts. Many of these biases and prejudices are implicit because of the worlds we move in and out of. Those worlds act as an echo chamber for our ideas, opinions, and actions. They are what many experts now refer to as "our bubble."

For example, I ask that we think about politics for a minute (a short minute). Recent research concludes that we tend to choose friends, cities, and urban or rural settings,[81] neighborhoods,[82] and overall living spaces that match our preferred political affiliation.[83]

---

81 Ryne Rohla, Ron Johnston, Kelvyn Jones, and David Manley, "Spatial Scale and the Geographical Polarization of the American Electorate," *Political Geography* 65 (2018): 117–122.

82 Benjamin Highton, "Sorting the American States into Red and Blue: Culture, Economics, and the 2012 US Presidential Election in Historical Context," *The Forum* 10, no.4 (February 9, 2013): 11–19, doi:10.1515/forum-2013-0002.

83 Alan I. Abramowitz and Kyle L. Saunders, "Is Polarization a Myth?" *The Journal of Politics* 70, no. 2 (2008): 542–555; Francis Fukuyama, "American Political Decay or Renewal: The Meaning of the 2016 Election," *Foreign Affairs* 95 (2016): 58.

Our political vote is by,[84] gender,[85] and even our technological savviness and exposure.[86] Ok, now stop thinking about politics. It was just an example to illustrate how social identity can fuel certain biases and prejudices.

Our next step is to identify those elements from our identity map that may influence our leadership style. Hannum recommends the following exercise.[87] Looking at the words we wrote on our identity map, underline those elements that are relevant as a defining core. Think about it and write down those words that define you and contribute to your uniqueness as an individual person. What are those things that would resent losing? Those words that define you more than any other? Do you see any trends in the words you underlined? Is there a common theme or pattern? How do those elements fit into your organizational culture and with your leadership style? For example, if I were to look at my identity map, I might note certain underlined words such as Spanish or European (both in my given identity), Christian and Catholic (both in my given and chosen circle), and humble and inclusive (at my core circle). I was raised in Spain as a Catholic and choose to practice Catholicism because it promotes humility and inclusion. Therefore, in my everyday life, my leadership style reflects my need to include diverse individuals and reach out

84 Brenda Major, Alison Blodorn, and Gregory Major Blascovich, "The Threat of Increasing Diversity: Why Many White Americans Support Trump in the 2016 Presidential Election," *Group Processes and Intergroup Relations* 21, no. 6 (2018): 931–940.

85 Kathleen Dolan, "Gender Stereotypes, Candidate Evaluations, and Voting for Women Candidates: What Really Matters?" *Political Research Quarterly* 67, no. 1 (2014): 96–107; Nicholas A. Valentino, Carly Wayne, and Marzia Oceno, "Mobilizing Sexism: the Interaction of Emotion and Gender Attitudes in the 2016 US Presidential Election," *Public Opinion Quarterly* 82, no. suppl_1 (2018): 213–235.

86 Jacob Groshek and Karolina Koc-Michalska, "Helping Populism Win? Social Media Use, Filter Bubbles, and Support for Populist Presidential Candidates in the 2016 US Election Campaign," *Information, Communication, and Society* 20, no. 9 (2017): 1389–1407; Gunn Enli, "Twitter as Arena for the Authentic Outsider: Exploring the Social Media Campaigns of Trump and Clinton in the 2016 US Presidential Election," *European Journal of Communication* 32, no. 1 (2017): 50–61.

87 Hannum, *Social Identity: Knowing Yourself, Leading Others*, 15.

for different points of view during meetings or projects. I usually face success with humility, giving credit to those who made it possible for my team and me to succeed. My motivation to work is usually not recognition, but successful collaboration and my own development. As a chronic learner, I accept that I do not have all the answers and that I can always get better at whatever I do. I have a strong belief in reflection and education (probably the Jesuit influence of my years teaching at Regis University).

Hannum recommends that we now add a plus sign to those factors (underlined words) that we believe positively affect our leadership style within our organization and a minus sign to those elements that negatively impact it. It is important to think about the factors on our identity map in the context of the organizational culture and environment. Now, after adding the pluses and the minuses, to better understand our identity map within the context of the organizational culture, we need more reflection. Here are some questions that you should ask yourself:

Are there any trends or patterns among those pluses and minuses? Can we see some of those factors reflected in the organizational culture, our management team, or our overall team?

- Do we see any potential conflicts?

- Can we identify any corporate traditions or way of working that support or contradict those elements?

- Are there any aspects of our social identity we would rather keep hidden in our business environment when engaging with our peers, coworkers, employees, shareholders, and customers?

- Are we displaying any recurrent behaviors or actions that feel in conflict to our core or chosen identity?

- Can we see how our given identity could favor us in certain projects within the organization? With certain personnel?

- Could our given identity be detrimental to our growth within the organization? Why? How?

- Does it hurt us with any specific corporate subgroup?

- How do we feel when we have to hide certain elements of our identity? Or how do we feel when we have to display behavioral elements that are not part of our identity map in order to fit the corporate culture?

Are we expecting members of our team to fit into certain profiles or display elements from our own social identity to succeed? And more importantly, is that expectation fair to them, necessary for the job to be completed, or just a tradition that could be written off?

Finally, let me close by stating that many of the social identity elements are linked to the previously discussed issues of dominant culture, power, and privilege. While we are going to avoid the larger discussion of privilege, we need to understand that we are even less aware of our privilege than we are of our biases and prejudices. And it is also important to understand the role that those privileges play in the way we behave. For example, being a tall white middle-aged Christian male means that when I walk into a meeting, my presence will have a certain effect on the participants. The effect will vary depending on the context, but overall, in the Western corporate world, my physical appearance and social identity are in my favor. I may not be aware of those privileges because they are potentially those elements expected from my in-groups, but it does affect the way others interact with me as much as the way that members of my in-group treat me. In my case, I became fairly aware about my physical appearance and social identity when my family and I moved to Beijing, China. It was difficult not to stick out among the crowd. The way I was treated, mostly to my advantage as a foreign visitor (unless I tried to bargain while shopping), was a result of my appearance.

In another example, my lighter skin gave me a certain advantage in different situations. For example, after 9/11, security increased substantially at airports. One new security process involved choosing individuals "at random" (and the quotes are done in purpose), as passengers were boarding the plane. My good friend and marketing director, Paco, and I used to fly together frequently. And I did love boarding the plane with him. You see, Paco is Mexican and, while he would be considered on the lighter skin side in Mexico, compared to me, he is seen as having a darker skin and he also wore a goatee and dressed casually when traveling. As we boarded the plane together, I could be certain that the TSA would pick him over me for an additional security check. He would get stopped and I will board without a problem. My physical appearance, in this context – boarding the plane, had a favorable result for me.

As we become aware of our identity map, we should be able to (1) improve our own self-awareness, (2) analyze and understand our leadership style, (3) contrast our leadership style with the organizational culture and examine the compatibility of both, (4) understand why we may feel exhausted after a day at work (to work against our autopilot or the elements of our identity map is an energy zapper), and (5) identify those elements from the identity map that may fuel some of our biases and prejudices.

PART II

A SHORT INTRODUCTION TO THE CHALLENGES OF OUR GLOBAL COMPLEXITY

THE GROWING COMPLEXITY

Journeying through the VUCA World

We live in a growingly complex world. Social, technological, environmental, political, economic, and legal challenges contribute to a surge in global and local complexity.[88] Contributing factors include changing consumer trends and preferences; societal pressures to change the role of corporations and governments; the challenges resulting from the dichotomy between retail and online businesses; the emergence of new business models; the economic turmoil in emerging markets (currency devaluations, dismantling the work of failed leftist populist governments); economic turmoil in developed countries (the emergence of a right-wing populist market, Brexit, the economic and social pressures on governments to reduce income inequality and adjust pensions to lower birth rates, the conflicting views on Middle Eastern and African migration); global trade trends shifts; and the misalignments between current workforce skills and future needs.

And then you have changes in technology such as the Internet of things (IoT), which is the interconnection of all things, machines, people, and smart devices through the Internet, collecting billions of bits of data per day. Artificial intelligence is another challenge. *Reuters News* reported that during 2018, more robots were put to work in Western countries than people. Little robots may soon deliver our pizza, and many repetitive assembly line jobs have already

---

88 Bob Johansen and James Euchner, "Navigating the VUCA World," *Research-Technology Management* 56, no. 1 (2013): 10–15.

been replaced by robots.[89] Some economists calculate that about 85 percent of the job losses blamed on globalization was a consequence of robotization and not replacement by cheaper labor in another country. To truly get an idea of what we are talking about, I would strongly recommend that you watch the special series "*Planet Money's T-Shirt Project*" (https://www.npr.org/series/248799434/planet-moneys-t-shirt-project). Researchers argue that the upcoming Fourth Industrial Revolution will shear the fabric of our society, changing the way that we interact with one another.[90]

Those are just a few factors that contribute the complexity of our business world. They introduce a sea of challenges that affect every day business operations and cannot be ignored by organizations. While this is not the topic of this book, this global complexity results in organizational pressures. In my previous research, I found that those organizational changes and the frequency and intensity of those changes result in higher levels of incivility, organizational cynicism, employee burnout, toxic behaviors, and other types of organizational trauma.[91]

Bob Johansen and the VUCA World

---

89 Bowler, Tim. "Will Globalisation Take Away Your Job?" BBC News. February 01, 2017. Accessed April 25, 2019. https://www.bbc.com/news/business-38600270. Stokes, Bruce. "First They Came for the Immigrants, Then They Came for the Robots." Foreign Policy. July 12, 2018. Accessed April 25, 2019. https://foreignpolicy.com/2018/07/12/first-they-came-for-the-immigrants-then-they-came-for-the-robots-jobs-manufacturing-labor/.

90 Klaus Schwab, "Globalization 4.0, a New Architecture for the Fourth Industrial Revolution," January 16, 2019, https://www.foreignaffairs.com/articles/world/2019-01-16/globalization-40.

91 Juan-Maria Gallego-Toledo, "Organizational Trauma and Change Management," in *Impact of Organizational Trauma on Workplace Behavior and Performance* (Business Science Reference, 2016), 140–161; Juan-Maria Gallego-Toledo, "The Relationship Between Perceived Frequency of Change and the Well-Being of Telecom Professionals" (PhD diss., The University of the Rockies, 2015).

In the late 1990s, Bob Johansen came up with the concept of the VUCA World.[92] VUCA stands for *Volatile, Uncertain, Complex, and Ambiguous.* Do those words describe the world we live in? While the concept itself did not gain full acceptance until after the 9/11 events in the United States, it truly became part of the Main Street business lingo after the economic crisis of 2008–9. When the concept was first introduced at the US Army War College,[93] it referred to a rapidly changing battlefield where the threats quickly metamorphosed, outdating existing tactics and requiring quick and creative in-the-field responses to achieve the main objectives. The central idea of the VUCA world is that the only certainty is the uncertainty and complexity of the world we are dealing with.

To allow for the flexibility and agility required in this new context, the field officers (or managers, directors, sales, etc.) need a clear vision to fulfill, along with the flexibility to decide how to reach such vision, also referred to as the commander´s intent. The individual in the field is provided with the purpose of the mission—take that hill—but, as she knows best the local conditions and the present context, she will decide how to accomplish the mission.

Bob Johansen also referred to the *command by negation.*[94] When faced with a goal, the individual in the field develops a plan and tactics. That plan is sent up the chain of command with the idea that it will be implemented unless the individual in the field hears otherwise. This concept allows the individual in the field, who knows the local conditions and context, to make the best tactical decisions in the present while the higher-level authority focuses on

---

92 Paul Kinsinger and Karen Walch, "Living and Leading in a VUCA World" (Thunderbird University, 2012).

93 Kirk Lawrence, "Developing Leaders in a VUCA Environment" (Executive Development, UNC Kenan-Flagler Business School 2013): 1–15.

94 Bob Johansen, *The New Leadership Literacies: Thriving in a Future of Extreme Disruption and Distributed Everything* (Berrett-Koehler Publishers, 2017).

developing and planning for the bigger picture, or the organization's ultimate goal.

While individual biases and our volatile, uncertain, complex, and ambiguous world present challenges to leadership, strategies such as self-awareness, organizational practices, and knowledge of how the complex world affects organizations can provide solutions. We need to engage our teams in dialogues, surveys, and conversations that uncover individual biases. We also need to understand that as a leader is that there is a difference between our intent and our impact. As leaders, we may have a certain message in mind, but we must have the necessary emotional intelligence to be aware of how the message have an effect on our audience.

Emotional intelligence is a term that grew in popularity from the work by Daniel Goleman. In his work, Goleman argued for the need to develop one's self-awareness, social awareness, or the awareness of others. Emotional Intelligence can be developed and is only moderately related to intelligence quotient (IQ). Goleman explained that leaders had to learn to manage the domains of emotion intelligence, such as self-awareness, self-management, and social awareness or relationship management.[95] We know what our intent was, but only by asking or having enough emotional intelligence do we know what the impact is on the other party.

The VUCA Prime—Flipping the VUCA World

An example of a current challenge for organizations in Europe is Brexit. As I write this book, the British Parliament has not accepted Prime Minister Theresa May's proposal for a soft exit (aka, a structured exit of the European Union) with only twenty-nine days left. This

---

95 Daniel Goleman, Richard E. Boyatzis, and Annie McKee, *Primal Leadership: Unleashing the Power of Emotional Intelligence* (Harvard Business Review Press, 2013).

means that, for example, British-owned airlines are not certain if they will be able to operate hundreds of flights within the European Union. All flights from British Airlines will have to generate or conclude in the United Kingdom (UK) unless an agreement is reached. This includes air transport of goods and people. Those goods are part of the logistics chain for many companies on both sides of the channel.

It is unclear what the British government's vision is for the new United Kingdom, lacks clear direction for where the politicians are trying to go. I would further state that it is even unclear what the people that voted to leave the European Union had in mind when they did so. Understanding the concerns of the Yes voters would clarify a way through the current political impasse. Still, the government needs to remain agile and flexible to adapt to the new reality. For example, while half of the government is against holding another referendum on leaving or not leaving the European Union, a solution could be found in conducting a referendum on the proposed Brexit deal. Are those terms satisfying the Yes voters? Do they address the concerns and reasons for the desired break?

Johansen argued in his research that the alternative to the VUCA world is a world where we use *vision* to demystify the *volatility* of our environment, *understanding* to tackle the *uncertainties*, *clarity* to address the *complexity*, and finally, *agility* to prepare for the *ambiguous* context in which we are submerged.

Clarity is the solution to the world complexity we face, and vision mitigates the volatile aspect of the VUCA world. The leader is expected to communicate a clear vision and set of goals. Through clarity, we make a deliberate effort to make some sense of the chaos.[96] Of course, communication requires a leader to customize his or her message to meet the expectations of a diverse audience. Clarity

---

96 Paul Kinsinger and Karen Walch, "Living and Leading in a VUCA
    World" (Thunderbird University, 2012).

of that communication is achieved by understanding one's audience. How does the audience prefer to have the message delivered? What level of detail should the leader provide? How technical should the message be? What specific words do most of the audience understand, and how can the leader reach the minority?

When delivering a message to the global workforce, what additional steps should be taken to ensure that the audience decodes the message in the closest way to its intent? While we as leaders may know our intentions, we cannot be certain of the impact our words will have unless we know the audience well and we receive feedback shortly after the message is delivered.

Johansen introduces the concept of *Smart-Mob Organizing*, defined as "the ability to bring together, engage with, and nurture purposeful business or social-change networks through intelligent use of electronic and other media."[97] In our previous example about Brexit, British politicians have failed to bring together the network of economists, politicians, sociologists, and other experts to develop a suitable solution to the current crisis. Instead of using technology to bring all that talent together, Prime Minister Theresa May is going at it (the Brexit agreement) alone, not tapping into the amazing diverse talent that the United Kingdom has.

As leaders, we need to be omnipresent in the organization using technology (i.e., social media, video conferences, email, voice mails) and smart traveling (i.e., appearances in key events to promote the vision with a customized message for the audience).

Future leaders need to interact with as many stakeholders as possible, constantly, instantly, and continuously in a productive and effective manner. Technology and social media makes this possible nowadays. The definition of a stakeholder is any group or individual

---

97 Johansen, *The New Leadership Literacies*, 101.

that is affected by the existence of the organization, its products or services, and hence, goes beyond the customers, shareholders, and employees. A two-way, ongoing active communication is needed and could be pursued through an open dialogue using social media or a physical town hall-style meeting. A leader needs to have her pulse on any individual or group that could influence the company's ecosystem.

Is the VUCA World Good or Bad?

Before we move forward on how volatility, uncertainty, complexity, and ambiguity affect leadership, please allow me to clarify one important point. The VUCA elements are not bad or good. Complexity is the opposite of simplicity, which not either good or bad in itself. It is a description of the situation we are facing.

Research shows that, in general, and despite the threats of climate change, we live in a better world now than we did decades ago. Progress over the last decades has been steady and overall beneficial. This is backed up by facts and statistics. For more of this, I recommend reading two recent books by psychologist Steven Pinker (*Enlightenment Now)* and sociologist Hans Rosling and colleagues (*Factfulness*). Despite what we see in the news, when we compare the past to the present, we find that poverty has gone down significantly; the middle class has grown globally to almost 75 percent of the world's population; we have fewer wars; life expectancy has grown in most countries; despite wild fires, we have more trees in Western countries than we did before; we are better prepared to eradicate disease epidemics; and there are fewer autocrats and dictatorships out there now than thirty years ago.[98]

---

98   Steven Pinker, *Enlightenment Now: the Case for Reason, Science, Humanism, and Progress* (Penguin, 2018); Hans Rosling, Anna Rosling Rönnlund, and Ola Rosling, *Factfulness: Ten Reasons We're Wrong about the World—and Why Things are Better Than We Think* (Flatiron Books, 2018).

So why do we think the world is worse than ever? It is partially due to the impact of two examples of biases—*stories preference* and *negativity bias*. First, our brain loves a good story more than it does numbers. We connect with the emotions and the messages of stories. They take us back to the oral traditions. Research shows that as leaders, one of the best ways to build our executive brand and connect with our audience is by using stories. Statistics and numbers do not generally solicit emotions. Why do you think nonprofit organizations usually show the picture of one single child or one hurt parent? Studies have shown that individuals are most likely to donate money when the story is personal. If the campaign includes the family of the child, the amount that an individual is willing to donate will decrease. If the advertising includes the stats of a whole country, the donor contributions are minimal. Telling a personal story allows the donor to relate to it, and it will have a bigger impact.[99] By the way, donations may increase if the child smiles or looks sad because the emotions tell a story. [100]

However, it's the negative stories that have the most impact. If the news tells you that one billion people were pulled out of poverty over the past two decades, it probably would not have a major impact on you. The news business has a negativity bias. It tends to report more negative events than positive. Still, my point is that life has grown more complex even though as a whole, we have made incredible progress over the last decades. Those terms could identify a potential opportunity as much as a potential problem.

99   CDB Burt and K. Strongman, "Use of Images in Charity Advertising: Improving Donations and Compliance Rates," *International Journal of Organisational Behaviour* 8, no. 8 (2005): 571–580; Sally Peter, "Should Charities Use Positive or Negative Empathy Appeal in Marketing?" *Medium* (blog) December 31, 2016, https://medium.com/@SallyPeter/should-charities-use-positive-or-negative-empathy-appeal-in-marketing-9c19a687c206.

100 Elaine Hatfield, John T. Cacioppo, and Richard L. Rapson, "Emotional Contagion," *Current Directions in Psychological Science* 2, no. 3 (1993): 96–100.

Vertical Development

Taking into consideration the challenges that leaders are facing now, we need to develop more than our skills and competencies, what we call horizontal development. Horizontal development is the most popular way to develop our employees – we need to teach a new task, take a course that teaches us how to accomplish such endeavor. We need to shift from the quick and analytical what-to-think problem solving approach to a longer-term critical thinking approach of how-to-think. That how-to think approach involves seeking different perspectives, engaging in new challenges and reflecting on the results and ways to improve in the future.[101] This requires shifting mentality and questioning assumptions. Asking questions such as "what do I believe in?" or "how could I be wrong?" allows us to focus on the essential meaning of our needs, instead of assuming what we or others need. Try listening to the emotions in yourself and others. Many of our behaviors, such as choosing a new car, hiring a new employee, or selecting a business strategy, are driven by emotions, which we then rationalize to sound more logical. What emotions are driving us to make decisions?

Consequently, dealing with dilemmas requires leaders to develop a different approach than the previous problem-solving approach. In the VUCA world, leaders are required to increase their focus on vertical development. Vertical development refers to the human development that we must earn for ourselves.[102] This type of development requires a great deal of self-awareness as well as an honest desire to change. Leaders must desire to grow into better leaders. And the main reasons lie in the VUCA world and the need

---

101   Radha Raghuramapatruni and Shanmukha Rao Kosuri, "The Straits of Success in a VUCA World," *IOSR Journal of Business and Management (IOSR-JBM)* (2017).

102   Nick Petrie, "Future Trends in Leadership Development," (white paper 5, no. 5, Center for Creative Leadership, Greensboro, NC, 2011).

to rely on others to succeed, expand our networks, tap into others´ expertise, and develop the agility to roll with the punches. Vertical thinking requires that as leaders, we develop more sophisticated ways of thinking, bring in different perspectives, and seek opportunities to try new ideas, make mistakes, learn from those mistakes, and expand our thinking.[103]

Because of the complexity we face, we need to seek the best solutions instead of searching for permanent solutions. As things are evolving and we are facing new challenges, permanent solutions are not possible because the *right* solution may not exist or be prohibitive from a time or cost perspective. Good enough will suffice in most situations—do not wait for a silver bullet, but do maintain the flexibility to adjust as you move forward. An excellent example of this approach can be seen in most current technological solutions. As consumers, we have come to accept that all software and most technology we buy, even cars, will require updates. If we were to wait for the perfect solution, we would not have access to some of the current technologies.

With that in mind, leaders must develop a clear understanding of the situation to neutralize the elements of uncertainty. Diversity plays a major role here; leaders need to listen to fresh perspectives and tap into many sources to make sense of a chaotic situation. Developing the agility to match the ambiguity is paramount in these VUCA scenarios. Johansen introduced research in his book *The New Leadership Literacies*, postulating for the need to move from the traditional centralized organization to a more "distributed everything," to become a shape-shifting organization.[104] Johansen borrowed the concept of shape shifting from his colleague Paul Baran and

---

103 Nick Petrie, "The How-To of Vertical Leadership Development–Part 2: 30 Experts, 3 Conditions, and 15 Approaches," (white paper, Center for Creative Leadership, Greensboro, NC, 2015).

104 Johansen, *The New Leadership Literacies*, 62.

the development of *packet switching*. In his "Future Now" blog at the Institute of the Future, Johansen explained shape shifting using these words:

> As Paul Baran described it to me, he was asked when he was at RAND to help create a telecommunications network that would resist nuclear attack. This was in the midst of the Cold War. At that time, networks were centralized, so if an enemy attacked any portion of it, the entire network could become vulnerable. In the new architecture, instead of centralized switching, packets were separated as they were sent and then put back together again when they were delivered. Paul Baran first described this as "hot-potato routing" but it came to be called packet switching, which made it possible for the network to continue working even if a portion of it was destroyed. [105]

In layman's words, we cannot resist organizational change but invite it to better respond to the changes in our context. We need to understand that our current vision and mission, for example, may change in two to three years. Before our VUCA world, a vision might have been developed and remained untouched for twenty to thirty years. Now, we need to adapt our approach to the market but ensure the creation of agile organizations. As organizations change, the role of employees must change as well, requiring the organization to provide them with flexibility to request a new set of skills, abilities, and knowledge to feed the change.

As change occurs, we need to lead. As leaders, we need to effectively communicate across people and organizations in real time, listening well to the feedback provided from different perspectives within the organization and the market. While the organization cannot (and should not) be controlled, it can be guided. The growth

---

105   Bob Johansen, "Leaders: Do You Know How to Lead Shape-Shifting Organizations?" The Institute of the Future, *Future Now* (blog), November 17, 2017, http://www.iftf.org/future-now/article-detail/leaders-do-we-know-how-to-lead-shape-shifting-organizations/.

along the edges results in a flourishing diversity, which a leader can exploit for the benefit of the organization. Leaders of a shape-shifting organization need to think divergently, using agility to understand other points of view, setting up incremental dividends of our investment in people and neutralizing one´s biases that would dismiss or block those divergent solutions.

In a complex world, we will not have all the knowledge necessary to address the challenges we face. We need to able to tap into the talent within the organization and outside the organization. The value that we create for customers depends on what resources we use from the company´s diverse workforce from collaborators (suppliers, logistic partners), customers and the communities we serve. These leaders need to develop their social networks to exploit the insights of the many, crowdsourcing for solutions throughout the organization. Part of this networking requires leaders to foster long-term interpersonal relationships to maintain their pulse on the multiple nodes within the organization.[106] Those long-term interpersonal relationships should be as diverse as possible to cultivate divergent opinions. Research shows that diversity leads to better outcomes.[107] After all, diversity is the best gate to creativity, and ultimately, leads to agile decision-making and a better understanding of the complex situation.

A word of caution about shape-shifting organizations—they can go tribal. We have defined *Tribe* as a community that develops a common set of traditions, norms, values, and behaviors. Going tribal means the isolation of certain communities from others, relying on in-group resources and limiting the access to outside groups. We all know subcultures that developed within one organizational culture.

---

106   Johansen, *The New Leadership Literacies*, 135.

107   Scott E. Page, *The Difference: How the Power of Diversity Creates Better Groups, Firms, Schools, and Societies* (Princeton University Press, 2007).

We have all heard in meetings variations of "this is how things are done here" or "in other organizations, it may work like that, but here, we do it differently." As Johansen noted, "Tribes can bring people together, but tribes get dangerous when the strength of an in-group comes at the expense of others on the outside."[108]

A shape-shifting organization needs to have leaders that have great levels of self-awareness. Those leaders have to learn to use the reach of social media and the Internet efficiently to lower barriers to group interaction by establishing two-way communication to secure the flow of fresh perspectives.[109] Geographies, physical location and time zones should no longer be barriers to communication. Leaders need to explore creative ways of gathering together to autonomously accomplish the objectives that would move the organization closer toward its common goal.

In conclusion, let us understand that no one leader has the answers to all the new challenges in the VUCA world. Agility is the best answer to the rapidly changing complex and ambiguous environment in which we now operate. Agility should be a natural component of teamwork. Organizations are turning to teamwork to address this complexity, and the global trend toward reliance on physical and virtual teamwork is intensifying.[110] Collaboration is taking up more of an employee's time than ever before because organizations expect teamwork to yield greater success through improvements in creativity, effectiveness, and productivity.[111]

---

108   Johansen, *The New Leadership Literacies*, 73.

109   Clay Shirky, *Here Comes Everybody: the Power of Organizing Without Organizations* (Penguin, 2008).

110   Marc Kaplan, Ben Dollar, Veronica Melian, Yves Van Durme, and Jungle Wong, "Shape Culture," in *Human Capital Trends 2016, Deloitte Insights*, deloitte.com/us/en/pages/human-capital/articles/introduction-human-capital-trends.html.

111   Christina N. Lacerenza, Shannon L. Marlow, Scott I. Tannenbaum, and Eduardo Salas, "Team Development Interventions: Evidence-Based Approaches for Improving Teamwork," *American Psychologist* 73 (4), 517.

Research shows that a team's success is often linked to its member composition.[112] The work produced by diverse teams usually results in more innovative companies that positively impact the organization's overall competitiveness through diverse, challenging, and candid input from all team members.[113] Diversity within a team provides a natural exposure to different perspectives. Different perspectives forces all of us to challenge established assumptions and moves us to the realm of the unknown, the outside the box thinking. By listening to others' perspectives, we become more inclusive as an organization, validating all individuals. Validation improves self-efficacy and productivity, which in turn, improves the employee engagement and commitment to the organization. All this results in higher employee productivity, team innovation and organizational profitability.

Decision Making and Biases

Biases play a central role in our everyday decision-making process. For example, let's talk about hiring practices. Studies show that managers are less likely to hire women for engineering or science-based positions. For example, a study showed that men were twice as likely as women to be hired for STEM-related professions.[114] In different studies, job applicants' first names on their resume (for example, Greg or Emily versus Jamal or Lakisha) influenced the individual's chances of obtaining a job interview, potentially identifying the hiring manager's implicit racial biases.[115]

112 Christina N. Lacerenza, Shannon L. Marlow, Scott I. Tannenbaum, and Eduardo Salas, "Team Development Interventions: Evidence-Based Approaches for Improving Teamwork," *American Psychologist* 73 (4), 517.

113 Jennifer Feitosa, Rebecca Grossman, and Maritza Salazar, "Debunking Key Assumptions about Teams: the Role of Culture," *American Psychologist* 73 (4), 376.

114 Ernesto Reuben, Paola Sapienza, and Luigi Zingales, "How Stereotypes Impair Women's Careers in Science," *Proceedings of the National Academy of Sciences* 111, no. 12 (2014): 4403-4408.

115 Marianne Bertrand and Sendhil Mullainathan, "Are Emily and Greg More Employable than Lakisha and Jamal? A field experiment on Labor Market Discrimination," *American Economic Review* 94, no. 4 (2004): 991–1013.

Simple presence could influence an individual's performance. In two studies conducted in 1999, a math test was administered to a group of women as the control group. [116] Then, the same math test was administered to a group of women with men present who were taking the exam as well. The average grades of the women in the mixed-gender group were considerably lower compared to the control group (women only test). But it did not stop there. When Asian men joined the equation, the average grades of the women and the Caucasian men were negatively affected.

Two recent studies found that even trained health professionals such as counselors and psychotherapists are not immune to the effects of implicit racial bias. [117] The research showed a preference toward white and middle-class potential clients based on the tone and dialect of their voices on phone messages left asking for a first-time appointment. Those tones, dialects, and voices from perceived working class and/or African American potential had a detrimental effect in regard to receiving return calls from the psychologists and counselors in the study.

At the unconscious level, these preferences and mental operations have the potential to act as a filter during our simplification of a complex situation and become prejudices that interfere with our judgments. We refer to those unconscious preconceived reasons as implicit biases, defined by a colleague as an idea or opinion formed before having the evidence for its truth or usefulness. Xiao and his colleagues suggested that implicit or unconscious biases usually start

116 Joshua Aronson, Michael J. Lustina, Catherine Good, Kelli Keough, Claude M. Steele, and Joseph Brown, "When White Men Can't Do Math: Necessary and Sufficient Factors in Stereotype Threat," Journal of Experimental Social Psychology 35, no. 1 (1999): 29–46; Steven J. Spencer, Claude M. Steele, and Diane M. Quinn, "Stereotype Threat and Women's Math Performance," Journal of Experimental Social Psychology 35, no. 1 (1999): 4–28.

117 Heather Kugelmass, "Sorry, I'm Not Accepting New Patients, an Audit Study of Access to Mental Health Care," Journal of Health and Social Behavior 57, no. 2 (2016): 168–183; Lea Winerman, "Left Out," Monitor on Psychology 47 (9) (September 2016): 50–53.

in early childhood and are correlated to the exposure to the beliefs, and practices of one´s in-group culture.[118] Biases and prejudices are hence learned traits against one thing, person or group born of social reasons and not rooted in rational or logical reasons. Implicit biases are strongly correlated to the exposure to one´s in-group culture and could be difficult for an individual to consciously identify those implicit biases.[119]

---

118 Wen S. Xiao, Genyue Fu, Paul C. Quinn, Jinliang Qin, James W. Tanaka, Olivier Pascalis, and Kang Lee, "Individuation Training with Other—Race Faces Reduces Preschoolers' Implicit Racial Bias: a Link Between Perceptual and Social Representation of Faces in Children," Developmental Science 18, no. 4 (2015): 655–663.

119 Irena Stepanikova, Jennifer Triplett, and Brent Simpson, "Implicit Racial Bias and Prosocial Behavior," Social Science Research 40, no. 4 (2011): 1186–1195.

PART III

APPROACHES TO COMPLEXITY

Using the Power of the Teams

I was recently talking to a friend who enjoys running marathons. He was getting ready to run in a large marathon, and he mentioned a chip that the runners carry. I was curious about that. Instead of fighting the crowd to get to the front, he usually likes to start from the back because he gets motivated as he passes the slower runners. This also helps him avoid seeing the faster runners gaining a lead on him until the last kilometers. He explained that the chip activates his time once he crosses the starting point. The chip ensures that everyone, regardless of how far back they start the race, has an equal chance to win - your time starts counting when you pass the start line (not when the first runner starts the race) and stops when you cross the finish line.

We leaders are the chips for our teams. To be an inclusive leader, we need to equalize the team's ground rules. We should make sure everyone has a chance to participate. We need to make sure that we have processes in place that compensate for those that started further back in their professional marathon. We need to translate those personalities, skills, knowledge, experiences, and abilities into contributions toward achieving our goals.

We also should identify areas of development for each of our team members, how to challenge them and prepare them for other future endeavors so that when they move on, and we wish them good luck, we know we have done our best to prepare them and those are not just words. Therefore, the final practical part of this book will begin with the formation and development of those teams.

In a recent study by the Center for Talent Innovation, 9.2 percent of white-collar workers in companies with one thousand or more employees felt that their bosses had underrated their potential, and they believed that the undervaluing of their skills was due to biases.[120] Employees believed that the perception of their skills, abilities, and knowledge was distorted by their bosses´ biases, negatively affecting the engagement with the organization and, ultimately, the productivity of those employees.

It is important to understand that most biases work at the unconscious level and therefore, we are not aware of how those biases are affecting the contextual stories developing in our minds and to which we are reacting. When we make a biased decision, we are not aware that we are acting on a biased belief and much less aware of the flawed process by which we came to that biased conclusion. For example, left to autopilot, confirmation bias will push us to ignore any evidence that contradicts our preconceived ideas while embracing those bits of information that reinforce them. The anchoring bias will catapult certain ideas to the top of the list of things to consider while sinking other ideas to the bottom of the list. And even if we bring our unconscious bias to the conscious level, studies show that it is not enough to have awareness to avoid the interference of prejudice.[121] Awareness is part of the solution but not the whole solution on its own. Action is needed to complete the neutralization process. Biases can be neutralized by developing the right decision-making process at the organizational level.

While it may be difficult to de-bias individuals, it is easier to de-bias organizational processes. The first step toward neutralizing one´s biased decision is to use the power of many. Decisions made by one single leader are more likely to err on the biased side than those made by groups. But the right team needs to be built. Effective communication among the team members and its

---

120 Sylvia Ann Hewlett, Ripa Rashid, and Laura Sherbin, "How to Keep Perceived Bias from Holding Back Potential Employees," *Strategy+Business*, September 11, 2017.

121 Daniel Kahneman, Dan Lovallo, and Olivier Sibony, "Before You Make that Big Decision," *Harvard Business Review* 89, no. 6 (2011): 50–60.

leaders is critical. Research found that 70 percent of commercial flight accidents stemmed from poor communication and team-work.[122] Communication and teamwork are also necessary to avoid groupthink, previously defined as the tendency to support the idea that everyone seems to like, the least conflicting idea or the idea expressed by the perceived expert on the matter or the de facto decision maker, without considering all relevant angles or asking for challenging perspectives.

During a debate between Malcolm Gladwell, the Canadian journalist and award-winning author, and Adam Grant, Wharton pro-fessor, and popular TED speaker, two interesting studies were brought up.[123] First, team familiarity and communication affected the rate of surgeons' success. Regardless of the surgeon's experience, her rates of success improved when she had more hours of effective collabo-ration with a familiar team. Similarly, the teams of the financial plan-ners appeared to determine their investment success rates. When those financial analysts were hired away from their teams, it took an average of five years to return to the same levels of success unless they took their teams with them to the other companies.

To effectively tap into the power of the group when making decisions, Kahneman, Lovallo, and Sibony developed a twelve-ques-tion checklist. As leaders, we could use this list to challenge some of our preconceived ideas, remain open to all possibilities, and reveal erroneous assumptions. Based on my research and my own expe-rience as a consultant, I combined best practices and developed these sets of bias-challenging decision-making set of questions, which I suggest that group members ask each other:

---

122 Michael Leonard, Suzanne Graham, and Doug Bonacum, "The Human Factor: the Critical Importance of Effective Teamwork and Communication in Providing Safe Care," *Qual Saf Health Care* 13, no. suppl 1 (2004): i85–i90.

123 "Bonus: a Debate with Malcolm Gladwell," TED Worklife with Adam Grant, May 10, 2018, https://radiopublic.com/WorkLife/ep/s1!ad684.

1. Do we have any significant reason to believe that self-interests within the group are affecting the decision? How does the decision affect the individual team members?

2. What's at stake for the team in our decision? What's the hardest part about this decision? What's the best part about this decision?

3. Did any team member present a dissenting opinion? How do I know this is true? Did we implement the Tenth Man approach[124] to our decision-making process? Did everyone have a chance to think about the problem before coming together with the other team members? What other alternatives did we consider? Why did we dismiss those alternatives?

4. What assumptions did we make? During our diagnosis, did we delve enough into the actual problem? Are we sure that we are looking at the causes of the problem and not just the symptoms? What gaps in information did we fill? How was the issue framed? Did we create unnecessary limitations or assumptions? Are we sticking to the company's traditions, and are those traditions valuable guidance or are they constricting our decision-making process?

5. Let's put ourselves a year from now—what information might we wish we'd have?

6. Did we question the source of our data?

7. How did we come up with the story? Go back to question 5—did we oversimplify the issue by filling up missing

---

124 William Kaplan, *Why Dissent Matters: Because Some People See Things the Rest of Us Miss* (McGill-Queen's University Press, 2017).

information? In 1998 HBR article, Hammond, Keeney, and Raiffa recommend reframing the question in various ways to force us to approach the issue from different perspectives.[125] How the question was posed influences the way we approach and understand the issue. Question your narrative.

8. Are we anchoring our decisions on past successes or failures? Are we assuming that we can replicate past successes or avoid past failures?

9. Are we overconfident? Over optimistic? Build a case from the outside. Find the holes in the plan as if we were the competition. Are we assuming that the competition will not react? That the context will not change?

10. Did we consider a truly worst-case scenario?

11. Are we being reasonably cautious or overly conservative?

Refining Your Hiring Process

An anecdotal case study presents the extent to which our biases as leaders play a role in the hiring process. In the 1970s and 1980s, a small percentage of well-known and respected orchestras had female musicians. Several orchestras decided to start conducting blind auditions. A musician would audition behind a screen that that concealed their gender. After removing their shoes (women's high-heels sound different than men's dress shoes), the study showed

125 John S. Hammond, Ralph L. Keeney, and Howard Raiffa, "The Hidden Traps in Decision Making," *Harvard Business Review* 76, no. 5 (1998): 47–58.

that women had a higher chance of getting hired and promoted when the auditions were blind.[126]

Biases play a key role in most hiring processes. As we have heard many times, we usually seek to hire people that remind us of someone perfect for the job...ourselves. Our minds are unconsciously guided toward minimizing ambiguity and uncertainty and are attracted to the familiarity of a candidate.

Most of us have a decision-making bias for maintaining the organization's status quo and sticking to the familiar. Campbell, Whitehead, and Finkelstein commented on two traps common to our decision-making processes—pattern recognition and emotional tagging[127]. As we learned before, our brain seeks to find patterns to come up with the right action unconsciously. Gaps in information are filled by the familiar. At the same time, the memories we are tapping into to make decisions and find patterns have an emotion attached to them. Most memories are attached to emotions—it's like the reference number we use to pull those memories. Memories with a tagged emotion are stronger and last longer, and we tend to recall those emotional memories before any other memory, which may perhaps explain one some individuals find experiential investment such as an adventure vacation more valuable than physical purchases. Likewise, when we are seeking to hire an individual, our brains are going to try to place the person before us into a familiar emotional context. For example, a candidate may remind us of our cousin Vito. Depending on the types of memories that we have on our cousin Vito, those memories would either predispose us to like (in-group) or dislike (out-group) that individual. From that point, we

---

126   Claudia Goldin and Cecilia Rouse, "Orchestrating Impartiality: the Impact of 'Blind' Auditions on Female Musicians," *American Economic Review* 90(4) (2000): 715–741.

127   Andrew Campbell, Jo Whitehead, and Sydney Finkelstein, "Why Good Leaders Make Bad Decisions," *Harvard Business Review* 87, no. 2 (2009): 60–66.

will focus on justifying our initial predisposition. By the way, the initial reaction would happen within two-hundred fifty milliseconds of meeting that person.

We can address this by adjusting the hiring process to minimize those personal biases. The first step is the job description itself. In a study conducted by Rudman and Glick showed that job descriptions were written in a more masculine or feminized manner, favoring one gender versus the other and inducing the hiring party to do the same.[128] The job description may include words that we associate with a certain gender. For example, any words that imply nurturing might be perceived as more feminine. Words that reference strength or directness might be connected to masculine traits. Even more interesting, if a job description was feminized, the female candidates that had more stereotypical female traits (nice) had higher chances of obtaining the position than females perceived to have fewer specific traits.

To avoid using gendered-language in job descriptions, Iris Bohnet, the author of the book *What Works: Gender Equality by Design*, recommends that we review the job description, minimize the mandatory requirements (male candidates have a tendency to apply to jobs even when not meeting all the requirements while female candidates will not apply unless they meet all requirements) and eliminate the gendered words such as *supportive* and *collaborative* (perceived as female characteristics) or masculine-perceived words such as *ninja*, *rock star*, *superhero*, or *hacker*. [129]

---

128 Laurie A. Rudman and Peter Glick, "Feminized Management and Backlash Toward Agentic Women: the Hidden Costs to Women of a Kinder, Gentler Image of Middle Managers," *Journal of Personality and Social Psychology* 77, no. 5 (1999): 1004; Laurie A. Rudman and Peter Glick, "Prescriptive Gender Stereotypes and Backlash Toward Agentic Women," *Journal of Social Issues* 57, no. 4 (2001): 743–762.

129 Iris Bohnet, *What Works: Gender Equality by Design* (Cambridge, MA: Belknap Press, 2016).

Technology can help an organization neutralize job application wording. For example, the site *Gender Decoder for Job Ads* (http://gender-decoder.katmatfield.com) compares the wording in a job description to gender-coded words identified by different researchers. In addition, companies such as Gaplumbers and Textio, to name a few, are developing software programs that allow an organization to neutralize any biased language in job descriptions and during the hiring process.

Once we have neutralized the job application language, we should focus on the actual hiring process. Research suggests that the hiring decisions should come from the bottom and not from the top, that we should involve individuals familiar with the position. For instance, we should create a team of three to five individuals as the hiring panel. Those individuals should be familiar with the organization and the position but also include an employee from a different division or unit, if possible. Next, ask the hiring panel to work with HR to develop a job description that goes beyond a list of skills and abilities, minimizing mandatory requirements. It is important to base that description on a normal day in the life for whoever fills that position. Whom will she be interacting with? What skills and knowledge would we rely on her to have? Which skills are teachable, and which ones should she already have (i.e., when hiring an accountant, we expect them to know accounting)? What knowledge will we need to provide her with? What soft-skills does she need to have? How will we characterize the organization's culture, and do we have a subculture that the person will need to fit into as well? Will the candidate fit the organizational culture? What values do we expect that person to display to successfully achieve an organizational culture fit? Word of caution – you need to understand what the values and norms at the core of the organizational culture are. Trying to find an individual that would fit the organizational culture does not mean finding a "mini-me" or a duplicate of existing personnel. Research conducted by Cameron, Quinn, and other organizational culture expert show that an alignment in the core values of leadership and the organization would improve efficiency in the organization. If certain values are at the core of the organization and its success (i.e. Apple, USAA, Southwestern Airlines), we need to find candidates that fit those values since those cannot be taught. At the same time, if we are going through an organizational transformation, we may want to hire people that share those aspirational values.

Developing a deeper understanding of the position, beyond basic job requirements will help you determine the right fit for your organization. Based on the desired attributes we developed, the hiring panel, coordinated by the HR specialist, should come up with questions for a structured interview. Those questions should be weighted for easy grading. I like to ask people in similar positions or who have previously held that position, what questions they would ask, what are essentials and what would be a bonus? Once I have created the prioritized list, I like to run the list by the same people to ensure that I have correctly reflected what I heard, and finally, I run it by HR to ensure that I am representing all aspects of a the organization to the potential employee (for example, are the organizational values reflected in our questions?)

I also seek ways to include simulations that test some of the expectations for the position. For example, the ability of the candidate to lead a team during a crisis or give a presentation to a large audience or test their abilities to adjust to change. Make sure to challenge some of the assumptions and traditions that surround the position. Are those necessary? Do they make the position more effective, or are they creating unnecessary boundaries? Speak up.

Ask questions about those assumptions to get to the core reason, if it even exists.

Speak-Up Culture

One of the main challenges to inclusive leadership revolves around identifying the needs of our employees. Without hearing from individuals, it is very difficult to guess what everyone expects from the organization. On the same hand, the organizational culture may pre-dispose a certain social dialogue and interactions among employees. Those expectations may negatively affect the engagement of certain people. Hewlett, Rashid, and Sherbin argue for a Speak-Up culture to battle that distortion from bias that demotivates employees.[130] Through the research they conducted for the Center for Talent Innovation, six behaviors were identified to develop an organizational Speak-Up culture, a culture defined by inclusive leaders. In my opinion, a inclusive leader defines what a speak-up culture is in the organization and the speak-up culture needs an inclusive leader to make it happen. Let me explain.

First, an inclusive leader should ensure that everyone has a say. The leader should engage individuals from different positions and geographical locations (the company's other locations and people who originally come from other parts of the world) but also those individuals who may not be as vocal due to language barriers, cultural differences (i.e., your relationship with people with power or high-power distance), or personality (i.e., introverts versus extroverts).

As a second and related step, make sure participants' feel safe introducing novel ideas and contributing nontraditional or unproven solutions. When providing feedback, as a leader, we need to ensure that it is timely, concrete, and includes actionable comments.

---

130 Sylvia Ann Hewlett, Ripa Rashid, and Laura Sherbin, "How to Keep Perceived Bias from Holding Back Potential Employees," *Strategy+Business*, September 11, 2017.

A fourth step involves requesting feedback on our own decisions and behaviors—don't forget that our intent does not always guarantee the impact we have on other people. Get a clear idea of what that impact was.

As a leader, you cannot be in more than one place at a time. Delegating decision-making power to team members is necessary. Ensure that you provide the team with clarity of mission (remember the commander´s intent we addressed in the VUCA chapter?) and allow them, as a fifth step, to make certain decisions. Finally, make sure that you give credit where credit is due. Make sure that other individuals within the organization know that the success was a team effort and actively communicate those success stories during organization events and with senior management.

In conclusion, it is important to remember that as leaders, we are, above all, human beings. Being a human being comes with the luggage of a biased decision-making process. Our decisions will unconsciously be affected by our human side; we are going to favor people from our in-groups, people we know and with whom we share values and beliefs; we are going to believe that we are unbiased and know better and that we will not be making decisions for our benefit.[131] Let´s develop controls in our business operations that prevent or limit the role that individual biases could have in decision-making activities. We can take measures to partially neutralize biased decisions by channeling the power of teams and organizational processes.

---

131 Mahzarin R. Banaji, Max H. Bazerman, and Dolly Chugh, "How (Un) Ethical Are You?" *Revista Icade, Revista de las Facultades de Derecho y Ciencias Económicas y Empresariales* 62 (2004): 359–365.

LABELING

How Do We Get Past Labels?

For many years, I headed sales and marketing for Nokia, a large telecommunication equipment manufacturer, for several regions in Latin America. As most people in Latin America will tell you, Miami is the capital city of Latin America. Therefore, I frequently traveled to Miami to meet customers and for internal meetings. During one of those visits, a good friend and colleague invited me to lunch with an old school mate. John, my colleague, friend, and Cuban American, introduced me to Jaime, a long-time Miami resident. During our conversation, Jaime, a very energetic middle-aged lawyer, who talked as much with his hands as he did with his mouth, brought up the topic of race, then went into a ten-minute monologue on how African Americans were ruining Miami and other racist remarks (interestingly enough, he was using African Americans and Haitians interchangeably). As his tone elevated in typical Latin manner, an African American gentleman approached the table and tapped Jaime on the shoulder. Jaime looked up and with a huge smile, embraced the African American gentleman and engaged in a lively conversation in *Span-English* (a mix of Spanish, English, and Anglicism), exchanging pleasantries and setting up a family dinner for a later date.

As the African American gentleman walked away, John, with one hand over Jaime´s shoulder, asked him, "How could you talk so much trash about African Americans and then hug and have family gatherings with African Americans?"

Jaime, looking shocked and confused, looked over his shoulder to his departing friend and answered, "John, what are you talking about? Max [the African American gentleman] is not black... he is Cuban." Labels matter.

And the main reason labels matter is that, as we have seen before, we create our narrative tying together the events that we are exposed to. Our brain has an amazing ability to anchor our experiences to new experiences (sometimes correctly, sometimes not so much), relating the unknown to what we know. Here we run into an issue called the narrative fallacy.[132] When we are faced with new information, our brains develop links to past events and extrapolate what is happening now, or even scarier, what might happen in the future. We fill up any information gaps with our own knowledge, sometimes faulty assumptions, to reduce the complexity of the story. The cause of this reasoning is intrinsically (and unconsciously) connected to certain laws of human nature.[133]

The Laws of Human Nature

Robert Greene narrated these laws in his 2018 book, *The Laws of Human Nature*, a heavy six-hundred-plus page book that will definitely change the way you interact with others. He mentions three principles that guide many of our behaviors. First, we want to believe that we are autonomous individuals, acting on our own and making our own decisions. We also believe that our intelligence level is above average (a fallacy in itself because how can everyone's intelligence be above average, statistically speaking?). And finally, we believe that we are basically good and decent. These principles explain why it is difficult to negotiate with another individual. We tend to be egocentric negotiators that believe we know best, and we are acting in the best interest of all parties.

As leaders of an organization, we need to establish structures and processes to neutralize our natural tendencies. We should

---

132 Robert Greene, *The Laws of Human Nature* (New York, NY: Viking, 2018).
133 Robert Greene, *The Laws of Human Nature* (New York, NY: Viking, 2018).

implement a system that promotes psychological safety, candor, and minimizes the distortions of the human biases in all of us. Amy Edmondson defined psychological safety as "a shared belief held by members of a team that the team is safe for interpersonal risk taking."[134] As an inclusive leader, aware of your own biases, you need to invite members of your team to express opinions and feedback without the fear of negative consequences.

In addition to inviting employees to express concerns with new or existing, ideas, initiatives, or assumptions, an inclusive leader should acknowledge those contributions and incorporate them, when possible, to the team's discussion.[135] As human beings, we want to be included socially, appreciated by our superiors, and perceived as providing value to the organization. We want to feel like a valuable contributor to our teams. Social loafing is not a default human behavior—it is a learned behavior that results from experiencing disrespect and incivility and feeling unappreciated.

Furthermore, when individuals feel that their values and beliefs are being challenge, affecting their social status, this could result in a detrimental impact on their self-efficacy. Self-efficacy refers to "people's beliefs about their capabilities to exercise control over events that affect their lives," as defined by Albert Bandura.[136] Bandura believed that the self-efficacy could have a positive or negative effect on an employee's performance. Those effects were borne from interference with our cognitive, affective, or motivational processes. When employees believe that they are operating in an

---

134   Amy Edmondson, "Psychological Safety and Learning Behavior in Work Teams," *Administrative Science Quarterly* 44, no. 2 (1999): 350–383.

135   Ingrid M. Nembhard and Amy C. Edmondson, "Making it Safe: the Effects of Leader Inclusiveness and Professional Status on Psychological Safety and Improvement Efforts in Health Care Teams," *Journal of Organizational Behavior: the International Journal of Industrial, Occupational and Organizational Psychology and Behavior* 27, no. 7 (2006): 941–966.

136   Albert Bandura, "Regulation of Cognitive Processes through Perceived Self-Efficacy," *Developmental Psychology* 25, no. 5 (1989): 729.

unjust, exclusive, punitive, or limiting business environment, negative self-efficacy becomes a strong possibility. Employees that work in a *perceived* environment that undermines self-efficacy will most likely disengage from the organization, reducing productivity to the overall team. Actively disengaged or passively disengaged employees cost organizations in lost productivity (absenteeism, sabotage, demotivation, low morale of coworkers, the negative effects of organizational cynicism, the negative impact on customer satisfaction resulting in higher customer turnover), lost creativity, and legal costs.[137] Disengagement results in an increase in deviant behaviors such as incivility and violence in the workplace, as well as higher levels of burnout among employees.

Inclusive leaders should promote work engagement among employees. Engagement requires employees to be enthusiastically involved with the organization and passionately committed to it and their work. And having happy and engaged employees helps the bottom line. Herb Kelleher, cofounder and former chairman of Southwest Airlines, stated that the organization's first responsibility was toward its employees. If you keep your employees happy, your customers will be happy since business success is all about relationships. A happy customer is one that comes back for more, ultimately improving revenues and the long-term viability of the business and hence, creates value for the shareholder.[138]

---

137   Mark Attridge, "Measuring and Managing Employee Work Engagement: a Review of the Research and Business Literature," *Journal of Workplace Behavioral Health* 24, no. 4 (2009): 383–398.

138   Chuck Lucier, "Herb Kelleher: the Thought Leader Interview," *Strategy+Business*, June 1, 2004, https://www.strategy-business.com/article/04212?gko=8cb4f.

Procedural Inclusive Adjustments

One step toward this goal is to develop what the Center for Talent Innovation refers to as a Speak-Up Culture,[139] which we previously talked about (see *"Using the Power of the Teams"*). The idea is to implement inclusive practices in management. For example, if we look at culture as defined by language, religion, customs, and politics,[140] a series of easy process-based practices can support systematic inclusiveness. Let's take an easy one—language. Is your signage appropriate for the employee force's composition? Do you have HR reps that speak the major predominant languages within your organization? Do you provide the option to use computers with different keyboard layouts? Do you issue your organizational announcements in one single language or all major spoken languages within your workforce? Easy adjustments to make.

Religion is another aspect of culture that we can easily address. As an organization, do we recognize only Christian, Muslim, Jewish, or Hindu holidays, or do we provide our employees with religious days flexible to their religious practices? A friend once told me that they did not celebrate "the coming and going of the big JC" in the company she worked for, meaning they did not give days off for Easter or Christmas. Instead, the company provided all employees with "free hours" of worship that could be used at the employee's discretion.

Organizations need to be sensitive to nationality and other cultural customs. Customs include a variety of factors such as clothing, gender roles, work schedules, and other relevant elements. I will provide you with an example of such an occasion during one of my overseas projects in my native Spain. During Christmas time, there is

---

139 Sylvia Ann Hewlett, Ripa Rashid, and Laura Sherbin, "How to Keep Perceived Bias from Holding Back Potential Employees," *Strategy+Business*, September 11, 2017.

140 John S. Ricaud, "Auditing Cultural Diversity: Understanding and Embracing Cultural Differences Is Essential to Survival in a Global Economy," *Internal Auditor* 63, no. 6 (2006): 57–62.

tradition to provide employees with a basket of Christmas foods such as marzipan, deli meats, *turrón* (nougat), and other holiday foods. As it had been a particularly good year for the company, the management (I am pretty sure that it was the GM's idea) decided to give out a full *paleta de jamón serrano ibérico*, which in this case, refers to the front leg of Iberico-type pork. It is a delicacy, and we were all very happy to receive it...all but our Muslim coworkers, who did not eat pork for religious reasons.

I reached out to a representative from HR department (since I worked closely with a Turkish friend that was affected) to suggest that the company should issue vouchers to a local store for those employees that chose to forsake the leg of ham and would rather purchase their own goods. I also suggested that the *Christmas* baskets be renamed the *New Year* basket. Easy adjustments such as these can be extremely inclusive.

Psychological Safety

As leaders, we should aim to make our teams as creative, effective, and productive as possible by combining inclusiveness and psychological safety. Diversity is a growing trend as previously mentioned. Inclusion cannot occur without psychological safety, a concept introduced by Amy Edmondson, a professor at Harvard University Business School, in a study published in 1999.[141] Edmondson defined team psychological safety as "a shared belief held by members of a team that the team is safe for interpersonal risk taking,"[142] meaning that all team members feel safe to voice opinions to their management and colleagues.

---

141   Amy Edmondson, "Psychological Safety and Learning Behavior in Work Teams," *Administrative Science Quarterly* 44(2) (1999): 350–383.

142   Amy C. Edmondson, "Psychological Safety and Learning Behavior in Work Teams," *Administrative Science Quarterly*, 44(2) (1999): 350–383.

As leaders, we need to ensure that our employees feel comfortable speaking their minds. We need to be inclusive leaders and take advantage of the diversity that is increasingly defining our teams and organizations. By inviting team members to share their thoughts and expertise, we open our teams to a potential myriad of possibilities and new stops in our journey toward an inclusive organizational culture.

I like another definition Edmondson included in her latest book *The Fearless Organization: Creating Psychological Safety in the Workplace for Learning, Innovation, and Growth*. Edmondson wrote that team psychological safety was the "climate in which people are comfortable expressing and being themselves."[143] It is important to understand that team psychological safety is not the same as team cohesiveness, a prelude to groupthink and a potential sign of disengagement with the team and/or organization, in my opinion. Psychological safety involves an invitation to express a candid opinion, without fearing negative consequences.

Team psychological safety could not happen without leader inclusiveness. A study conducted in the health industry showed that an inclusive leadership style had a positive effect on the active participation of team members toward the quality improvement learning efforts.[144] As discussed earlier in the book, the changing environment in which we operate requires our teams to constantly update and improve through collective and individual learning. Since differentiation in service offering and value is of capital importance and the heterogeneity in our customer base requires our teams to customize

---

143 Amy C. Edmondson, *The Fearless Organization: Creating Psychological Safety in the Workplace for Learning, Innovation, and Growth* (Wiley, 2018).

144 Ingrid M. Nembhard and Amy C. Edmondson, "Making It Safe: the Effects of Leader Inclusiveness and Professional Status on Psychological Safety and Improvement efforts in Health Care Teams," *Journal of Organizational Behavior: the International Journal of Industrial, Occupational, and Organizational Psychology and Behavior* 27, no. 7 (2006): 941–966.

solutions to fit individual customers whenever possible, the combination of team diversity and an inclusive leadership style will be assets for any organization. Psychological safety is an essential component to inclusive leadership.

Kim S. Cameron and Robert E. Quinn introduced their Competing Values Framework in 1999, describing four types of dominant organizational culture.[145] It's a fascinating line of research that we do not have time to delve into, but I want to refer to one of their lessons. For an organization to be at its peak performance, the organizational culture needs to be aligned with the leadership culture. This alignment will support the dynamism of the team affected by the actions, behaviors, and perceived messages received from the leader. To add a bit of academic rigor to this concept, allow me to quote another aspect of the definition of leader inclusiveness according to Nemhard and Edmondson: "Words and deeds by a leader or leaders that indicate an invitation and appreciation for others' contributions."[146] A leader needs to invite contributions from the team members, acknowledge those contributions and incorporate them, when appropriate, into his decision-making process.

A team will take its cues from not just the behavior, actions, and words of a leader, but also from the other team members' reactions to those behaviors. Just as in regular communication, there is more to communication than our words—our body language, willingness to listen, acknowledgement of contributions, reactions to feedback, and a genuinely perceived invitation to participate will play a major role in the team's perception of inclusiveness.

145 Kim S. Cameron and Robert E. Quinn, *Diagnosing and Changing Organizational Culture: Based on the Competing Values Framework* (Jossey-Bass, 2011).

146 Nembhard and Edmondson, "Making It Safe: The Effects of Leader Inclusiveness and Professional Status on Psychological Safety and Improvement Efforts in Health Care Teams," 947.

Research shows that inclusive leaders need to build team psychological safety by applying a set of steps. First, open a dialogue with your team and other members of the organization and invite candid conversation. Ask them to challenge the current assumptions what Edmondson calls "framing the work."[147] Clarify and emphasize the team's goal, and make sure to ask open-ended questions without passing judgment. It is important that the team notices your willingness to listen. Two of the most effective ways to listen is to ask questions and to paraphrase meaningful and conclusive bits of the conversation to check for proper understanding.

During my time working in Latin America, I became frustrated with some of my direct reports' meeting management skills. We would agree on the agenda topics and set a timetable. While I expected some delays, I grew frustrated with how much time was wasted with personal conversations. We would arrive at the meeting and start late, and for the first hour, there would be more conversation about personal matters than work-related topics. After a month of such meetings, I decided it was time to change things.

The first thing I did was not define the agenda. By asking questions about the meetings and listening to the participants' answers, two patterns showed up in their feedback - we were choosing topics that were of no interest to the audience (meaning, irrelevant to some of the participants), and the agendas were too ambitious. I have never been a friend of brainstorming but rather use brainsteering,[148]

---

147   Edmondson, *The Fearless Organization: Creating Psychological Safety in the Workplace for Learning, Innovation, and Growth*, 155.

148   Kevin P. Coyne and Shawn T. Coyne, *Brainsteering: a Better Approach to Breakthrough Ideas* (New York, NY: Harper Business, 2011); Kevin P. Coyne and Shawn T. Coyne, "Seven Steps to Better Brainstorming," *McKinsey Quarterly* 2 (2011): 1–8.
Kevin P. Coyne and Shawn T. Coyne, "Seven Steps to Better Brainstorming," McKinsey Quarterly, March 2011, accessed April 25, 2019, https://www.mckinsey.com/business-functions/strategy-and-corporate-finance/our-insights/seven-steps-to-better-brainstorming.

a system developed by two McKinsey associates. Brainsteering is a seven-step process that helps participants collect relevant ideas, choose the right people, clarify expectations, split the team and then have each sub-team build on those ideas, merging those ideas afterward and ultimately arrive at a better conclusion without the dangers of groupthink or social loafing. This short description does not do justice to the concept so feel free to check the two sources provided below. By following the brainsteering process, it pushes participants to listen and be willing to incorporate all team members' ideas. You also reduce the potential impact of groupthink, since you start in sub-teams and it would be unlikely that every sub-team would come up with the same idea.

We used the brainsteering process to come up with relevant meeting topics as well as a potential timetable. We also determined that we would park any new topics that emerge during the meeting by writing them on a different flipchart and then either set up a separate meeting or add it to the next one. In addition, we scheduled time for personal sharing. We agreed that we would devote the first thirty minutes to catch up over coffee, lunch, or dinner. That way, the contributing managers felt they had the relationship-building time so important for Latins while respecting the work time. Thereafter, the meetings became more productive.

Two final ideas on psychological safety. First, failures will occur, and accountability is important. When failures happen, you need to ensure that the team learns from them. Psychological safety is not carte blanche to underperform without consequences. The team members need to feel accountable for the results but not afraid to take future risks.

During my seventeen plus years at Nokia, the Finnish organizational culture invited employees to try new things, take risks, and share what they learned. But we also were expected to learn from our errors and develop skills to close potential knowledge gaps. Just as I owned my failures, and I felt accountable, I was also praised when my efforts were successful. Second idea about a psychological safety practice, leaders need to regularly and publicly praise their teams and celebrate the small wins. This is particularly important when going through organizational changes or during long projects—make sure to pause to celebrate accomplishments regularly.

As we like to say at the Center for Creative Leadership, while we may know what our intent was, only the other party can tell us about the impact. As a leader, we can only worry about ensuring that our intent is as clear as possible through self-awareness, cultural intelligence, and projected psychological safety. We also need to have the procedural structure in place to support challenges, test assumptions, incorporate feedback, promote idea exchange, clarify requests, invite discussion on approaches or differences in opinions, or provide an incentive of additional contributions from team members. Team psychological safety is indispensable for bringing value through creativity, innovation, and performance to our customers and our employees in this fast changing VUCA world. Those systematic practices need to be part of the organizational culture. We need to cultivate a culture where a team member will speak up with confidence, trust, and respect for others. And leaders need to understand the impact of our actions. By facilitating the learning behaviors in work teams, we effectively address any changes or challenges without fear of interpersonal threats, to drive team performance.

USING ASSESSMENT TOOLS TO IMPROVE SELF-AWARENESS

Understanding Where We Stand

As I mentioned in the introduction, when I was an expat in China, I failed to train my Chinese colleagues on the importance of coaching. Despite pushing Nokia's statistics on the success rates of teams that regularly used coaching and mentioning the clear policies coming from Finland, I was only able to fully train a small fraction of the regional directors, and I was unable to convey the importance of coaching direct reports for future success. It was later that I realized I had acted without having enough cultural background and had assumed that the dominant culture was the Nokia organizational culture as was the case in most of the other divisions I had previously headed. The Nokia organizational culture called for a minimally hierarchical structure, a consensus and egalitarian decision-making process and an impulse to change and renew oneself throughout one's career. The organizational culture urged employees to challenge the status quo and think outside the box. Making mistakes was ok as soon as you learned from those and become a better person. Chinese culture (and I am generalizing) is more hierarchical, strongly based on Confucian principles of an obedience order to seek a harmonious solution. *Guanxi* defines a relationship between two individuals based on mutual respect, trust and harmony.[149] I later wrote an article about that experience and, in hindsight,

---

149 Kwock, Berry, Mark X. James, and Anthony Shu Chuen Tsui. "Doing business in China: what is the use of having a contract? The rule of law and guanxi when doing business in China." Journal of Business Studies Quarterly 4, no. 4 (2013): 56.

a more effective methodology that I should have used.[150] Having known about cultural intelligence and the assessments that I am about to introduce you to would have improved the odds of success with the Chinese executives.

Few business individuals will deny that executives and managers live in a globalized economy. While we could argue about the pros and cons of globalization and quickly spill over into a political debate (by the way, we choose our in-groups on those topics), the fact remains that our economy is more globalized now than ever before. In this globalized world, we are regularly faced with decisions that involved multicultural elements related to customers, suppliers, employees, and other stakeholders. The potential costs of intercultural misunderstandings and resulting mistakes are high. Those losses could include a decline in employee productivity; the slow reaction and delivery by an offended supplier; the loss of business from insulted customers; the lost creativity from disengaged employees; sabotage by customers; or the negative repercussions on sales from a cultural faux-pas. And let's not even get into the potential effects on our corporate social responsibility strategy—do we understand what our communities expect from us? How can our organization support the causes that matter and move away from the toxic topics? Most of these cultural gaffes result from biased opinions or assumptions and could be prevented by developing a higher cultural intelligence.

Christopher P. Earley affirmed that cultural intelligence (CQ) was a construct developed to improve the quality of intercultural interactions[151], or "a person's capacity to adapt to new cultural

---

150   Juan-Maria Gallego-Toledo, "Cultural Profiling and a Chinese Experience," *Journal of Chinese Human Resource Management* 6, no. 2 (2015): 120–132.

151   Christopher P. Earley, "Redefining Interactions across Cultures and Organizations: Moving Forward with Cultural Intelligence," *Research in Organizational Behavior* 24 (2002): 271–299.

contexts"[152] from three different perspectives—cognitive, motivational, and behavioral. CQ might be seen in the executive's ability to effectively communicate and interact with an individual from a different culture.[153]

Specifically, David C. Thomas and colleagues defined CQ as "a system consisting of cultural knowledge, cross-cultural skills, and cultural metacognition that allows people to interact effectively across cultures."[154] Basically, CQ refers to knowing the culture you are encountering as much as possible (i.e., asking questions, reading about the culture, asking other expats about their experiences...); having the skills to survive in such culture (knowing the do's and don'ts. For example, the cultural imperatives or practices you need to implement to succeed); and the evaluation of what is working and what is not? Hence, cultural intelligence focuses on an individual's ability to effectively interact with and succeed within a culturally diverse setting.[155]

When I first arrived in China, I was in charge of strategic planning for a large group of individuals. I decided to have a set of meetings to determine what stage of implementation of the latest Nokia organizational strategy the different teams were in. The Nokia organizational culture is based on a fairly flat organization where anyone

152 Early, "Redefining Interactions across Cultures and Organizations: Moving Forward with Cultural Intelligence," 274.

153 David C. Thomas, "Domain and Development of Cultural Intelligence: the Importance of Mindfulness," *Group and Organization Management* 31, no. 1 (2006): 78–99; David C. Thomas, Efrat Elron, Günter Stahl, Bjørn Z. Ekelund, Elizabeth C. Ravlin, Jean-Luc Cerdin, Steven Poelmans, et al., "Cultural Intelligence: Domain and Assessment," *International Journal of Cross-Cultural Management* 8, no. 2 (2008): 123–143.

154 David C. Thomas, Yuan Liao, Zeynep Aycan, Jean-Luc Cerdin, Andre A. Pekerti, Elizabeth C. Ravlin, Günter K. Stahl, et al., "Cultural Intelligence: a Theory-Based, Short Form Measure," *Journal of International Business Studies* 46, no. 9 (2015): 1099–1118.

155 Thomas Rockstuhl, Stefan Seiler, Soon Ang, Linn Van Dyne, and Hubert Annen, "Beyond General Intelligence (IQ) and Emotional Intelligence (EQ): The Role of Cultural Intelligence (CQ) on Cross-Border Leadership Effectiveness in a Globalized World," *Journal of Social Issues* 67, no. 4 (2011): 825–840.

can speak up and candidly provide feedback or ask questions. Several things happened during those first meetings that modified how I ran the meetings at Nokia China. First, I noticed that if I voiced my opinion first, it was the end of the debate—the participants would agree with me, and there would be no conversation. My opinion was perceived as the last word on the matter. I also noticed that after asking a question, the participants would take between three and five seconds to come up with an answer. Trying to rush them would only delay answers. Also, if any other foreigners were present, the Chinese colleagues would wait to hear what they had to say before commenting. I, therefore, started asking questions directly to individuals and waited patiently for answers.

Just to be clear, cultural intelligence (CQ) is not the same as the intelligence coefficient (IQ) or emotional intelligence (ECQ). In 2012, Linn Van Dyne and colleagues defined CQ as "an individual's capability to detect, assimilate, reason, and act on cultural cues appropriately in situations characterized by cultural diversity."[156] The research attests to the improvement of an executive's cultural capacity (the physical or mental power to take action in a different cultural environment) through the development and mastering of (a) the cognitive abilities (the head— understanding why people behave the way they do), (b) the emotional aspects of culture (heart—understanding the emotions behind the decisions), and (c) behavioral patterns (actions—identifying action patterns based on the cultural context).[157]

---

156 Linn Van Dyne, Soon Ang, Kok Yee Ng, Thomas Rockstuhl, Mei Ling Tan, and Christine Koh, "Sub-Dimensions of the Four-Factor Model of Cultural Intelligence: Expanding the Conceptualization and Measurement of Cultural Intelligence," *Social and Personality Psychology Compass* 6, no. 4 (2012): 295–313.

157 Brent MacNab, Richard Brislin, and Reginald Worthley, "Experiential Cultural Intelligence Development: Context and Individual Attributes," *The International Journal of Human Resource Management* 23, no. 7 (2012): 1320–1341.

Research conducted by McKinsey & Company found that managers that developed a better awareness of their own conscious and unconscious biases and prejudices developed an improved understanding of the effects those biases had on their professional decision-making processes. Improvements in self-awareness were correlated with a reduction in groupthink, overconfidence, or over-optimism and pushed executives toward a more direct reliance on hard data to make decisions.[158] In a globalized business world, effective cross-cultural leadership demands the development and understanding of the relevant four dimensions:

(1) Cognitive (cultural awareness, self-awareness, and knowledge) includes the knowledge of cultural beliefs, mores, practices, and customs that can facilitate understanding in a cultural situation.

(2) Metacognitive (developing, expanding, and using cultural knowledge) refers to the individual´s level of cultural awareness and her ability to recognize potential gaps in knowledge relevant to the immediate interactions.

(3) Motivational (perseverance, resiliency, and self-efficacy) builds on an individual's self-efficacy or her beliefs about her abilities to successfully engage individuals from other cultures.

(4) Behavioral (conscious behavior adaptation) defines a leader's ability for cultural adaptation.[159]

---

158 Tobias Baer, Sven Heiligtag, and Hamid Samandari, "The Business Logic in Debiasing," *McKinsey and Co.* (website), 2017, http://www.mckinsey.com/business-functions/risk/our-insights/the-business-logic-in-debiasing.

159 Earley, P. Christopher and Randall S. Peterson, "The Elusive Cultural Chameleon: Cultural Intelligence as a New Approach to Intercultural Training for the Global Manager," *Academy of Management Learning and Education* 3, no. 1 (2004): 100–115; Kay L. Gibson, Glyn M. Rimmington, and Marjorie Landwehr-Brown, "Developing Global Awareness and Responsible World Citizenship with Global Learning," *Roeper Review* 30, no. 1 (2008): 11–23; Linn Van Dyne, Soon Ang, Kok Yee Ng, Thomas Rockstuhl, Mei Ling Tan, and Christine Koh, "Sub-Dimensions of the Four-Factor Model of Cultural Intelligence: Expanding the Conceptualization and Measurement of Cultural Intelligence," *Social and Personality Psychology Compass* 6, no. 4 (2012): 295–313.

Let's move to the practical aspect of cultural intelligence. There are several research-supported techniques to assess, develop, and improve the metacognition ability, or mindfulness, by bringing implicit biases to a conscious level and using experiential methods for de-biasing. This means understanding what makes us tick and what we can do to address our hot buttons, those things that upsets us. Specifically, four assessments can provide our cultural intelligence level to improve our self-awareness.

Extended-Cultural Intelligence Scale

Full disclosure—I have participated in several certification courses from the following institutions, and I actively follow up with their research and the work that they do. I may be biased on the usefulness of their tools. That being said, the Cultural Intelligence Center (https://culturalq.com/), a Michigan-based company, developed a tool that I have found extremely helpful in cultural self-awareness. The Extended Cultural Intelligence Scale (E-CQS) includes thirty-seven items, including the previously mentioned four dimensions and an additional eleven subdimensions. The E-CQS measures the four dimensions that ascertain an individual's ability to manage themselves successfully within culturally diverse contexts. This tool has been validated over time as an effective assessment scale across samples, times, countries, and methods.[160]

The E-CQS measures cognitive CQ by assessing the subdimensions of Cultural-General Knowledge and Context-Specific Knowledge. The subscales of Intrinsic Interest, Extrinsic Interest, and Self-Efficacy determine motivational CQ. Three subdimensions—planning (strategizing before a culturally diverse encounter),

---

160 Soon Ang, Linn Van Dyne, and Christine Koh, "Personality Correlates of the Four-Factor Model of Cultural Intelligence," *Group and Organization Management* 31, no. 1 (2006): 100–123.

awareness (use of critical thinking and self-awareness), and checking (reviewing assumptions and adjusting to specific expectations) defines the Metacognitive CQ. Finally, Behavioral CQ is a construct of verbal behavior, nonverbal behavior, and speech acts subdimensions.[161] Speech acts refers to any message that serves a social function such as welcoming someone, apologizing, thanking someone. More information about the E-CQS can be found at https://culturalq.com/pricing-for-workplace/.

In addition to the E-CQS, the Cultural Intelligence Center offers a Cultural Values Profile that can be used to manage unconscious bias at the corporate level. The methodology includes the awareness part and also the systematic changes to reduce potential unconscious bias. Some of the recommended practices and procedures aim to incorporate fail-safe switches in different functions, particularly in the hiring, development and promotional areas of human resource management.

Intercultural Effectiveness Scale (IES)

The Kozai Group (https://www.kozaigroup.com) developed the Intercultural Effective Scales (IES). The IES (https://www.kozai-group.com/intercultural-effectiveness-scale-ies/) is a self-assessment survey composed of a fifty-two-item questionnaire on a Likert Scale (a scale used to measure attitudes or opinions) that measures an executive's global effectiveness. A global mindset is "the degree to which one is interested in and seeks to actively learn about other cultures and the people that live in them."[162]

---

161 Van Dyne et al., "Sub-Dimensions of the Four-Factor Model of Cultural Intelligence: Expanding the Conceptualization and Measurement of Cultural Intelligence"

162 Mark E. Mendenhall, Michael J. Stevens, Allan Bird, and Gary R. Oddou, "Specification of the Content Domain of the Global Competencies Inventory," *The Kozai Monograph Series* 1, no. 1 (The Kozai Group, 2008): 1–43.

The IES uses three scales: Continuous Learning [CL], Interpersonal Engagement [IE], and Hardiness [H]. It includes six sub-scales: Self-Awareness and Exploration under CL, Global Mindset and Relationship Interest under IE, and Positive Regard and Emotional Resilience under H. Many of these scales and subscales draw parallels between self-awareness as defined by the IES and the behavioral facet of CQ.[163]

The IES provides the basis for a plan. By analyzing your results, you are presented with potential areas of intercultural effectiveness you should address to improve your success when operating in multicultural environments. In addition to improving your cultural self-awareness, you are presented with an action plan to improve your global effectiveness.

Implicit Association Test (IAT)

Next, the IAT assessment gets to the nitty-gritty of personal biases, allowing us to identify those implicit prejudices, in theory. Allow me first to give you a bit of background on the IAT. But before you jump on your computer, read the criticism related to this assessment as well as the research backing it up. I find the research (on both sides of the aisle) energizing as I feel (notice I use "feel") that there is something here to be expanded upon. Unfortunately, this is a good example of academic tribal warfare, with one group focusing on supporting the IAT and another group targeting its destruction.

This topic has been studied at great depth by sociologists Mahzarin Banaji and Anthony Greenwald in their book *Blindspot— Hidden Biases of Good People*.[164] In their research, the two sociologists

---

163   David C. Thomas, "Domain and Development of Cultural Intelligence: the Importance of Mindfulness," *Group and Organization Management* 31, no. 1 (2006): 78–99.

164   Mahzarin R. Banaji and Anthony G. Greenwald, *Blindspot: Hidden Biases of Good People* (Bantam, 2016).

describe the hidden biases that we, social creatures, develop through exposure to cultural attitudes and the trends and patterns of our social groups. They developed an self-administered assessment tool, the Implicit Association Test in 1995. Their book details how they developed the Implicit Association Test (IAT) as a social behavior experiment to measure an individual´s implicit bias.[165] This free assessment was developed as part of Project Implicit (https://implicit.harvard.edu/implicit/aboutus.html), founded in 1998. The purpose of Project Implicit is to "educate the public about hidden biases and to provide a 'virtual laboratory' for collecting data on the Internet." The Implicit Association Test (IAT) was designed to study the implicit disconnect between intentions and actions (https://www.projectimplicit.net/index.html) and to quantify the strength of the associations between concepts and stereotypes.

As a leader, I would urge you to visit the Project Implicit site at https://implicit.harvard.edu/implicit/takeatest.html. After you read the first screen (Preliminary Information), click on "I wish to proceed," and you will be taken to a page with an array of assessments. The assessments (2017 and 2018 at the time of the writing of this book) included topics such as "Gender and the Career," "Race," "Arab-Muslim," "Age," "Asian," "Weight," "Religion," and even "Presidents."

Each test will take about seven to ten minutes to complete, and I suggest you complete as many as possible. The results will shock you. The assessments have been validated by a long list of researchers, from independent to the original researchers Banaji and Greenwald. Once you have completed a test, take several minutes to reflect on the results. Journal about your initial thoughts when you saw the results—what emotions you felt, reasons you thought they

---

165   Mahzarin R. Banaji and Anthony G. Greenwald, *Blindspot: Hidden Biases of Good People.*

were incorrect, reasons you thought they were right on the money. Can you think of any instances where something in the test results matched your workplace behavior? Can you think of any decision you've made that contradicts something in the results? Have you ever acted differently around an individual fitting the biased profile? Write down your answers before you take the next test. If something surprises you, confide on someone you trust, and share the results. Ask them for their opinions.

As previously stated, I want to maintain my goal of providing strong, research supported information and presenting differing points of view. With that in mind, I should mention that there is plenty of controversy regarding the IAT assessment in the academic world.[166] Many experts question the research the proponents of the assessment use to support its use, particularly, Banaji and Greenwald's work. [167] Arguments have been made that the IAT assessment was launched prematurely without completing the research to scientifically support the assessment's effectiveness. Some critics argue that the assessment lacks the necessary reliability (related to the amount of measurement error or consistency in results) or validity (does it measure what it is meant to measure) to support the measurement of implicit bias.[168] Finally, there is a group of critics who argue that a

---

166   Gregory Mitchell and Philip E. Tetlock, "Popularity as a Poor Proxy for Utility: the Case of Implicit Prejudice," in *Psychological Science under Scrutiny: Recent Challenges and Proposed Solutions,* eds. Scott O. Lilienfeld and Irwin D. Waldman (Wiley, 2017).

167   Hart Blanton, James Jaccard, Jonathan Klick, Barbara Mellers, Gregory Mitchell, and Philip E. Tetlock, "Strong Claims and Weak Evidence: Reassessing the Predictive Validity of the IAT," *Journal of Applied Psychology* 94, no. 3 (2009): 567; Frederick L. Oswald, Gregory Mitchell, Hart Blanton, James Jaccard, and Philip E. Tetlock, "Predicting Ethnic and Racial Discrimination: a Meta-Analysis of IAT Criterion Studies," *Journal of Personality and Social Psychology* 105, no. 2 (2013): 171.

168   Yoav Bar-Anan and Brian A. Nosek, "A Comparative Investigation of Seven Indirect Attitude Measures," *Behavior Research Methods* 46, no. 3 (2014): 668–688; Kristin A. Lane, Mahzarin R. Banaji, Brian A. Nosek, and Anthony G. Greenwald, "Understanding and Using the Implicit Association Test: IV," *Implicit Measures of Attitudes* (2007): 59–102.

high score on the IAT assessment could be correlated to the partici-pant's empathy for an out-group, as well as that individual's poten-tial familiarity with the negative stereotypes about that out-group and does not associate any unconscious bias toward it.[169]

From reading articles on both sides of the argument, I found that the principle objections to the validity of the IAT center around the ability of the assessment to predict discriminatory behaviors. There is an aspect of self-awareness that seems to go unchallenged: unconscious bias. In my opinion, there is a great value to be had by any leader in understanding his or her unconscious bias, regardless of acting (or not) on those unconscious biases.

From my research and experience, unconscious biases become more difficult to manage when the individual goes into autopilot because of lack of sleep, mental or emotional exhaustion, stress, or other reasons that can lower one´s behavioral inhibitions. Therefore, I still believe that the knowledge obtained through the IAT assessment could be valuable to any leader.

Culture-Influenced Behaviors

As mentioned, many of our behaviors are anchored in our cul-tural backgrounds. We behave in ways that reflect our beliefs and those are constructed on the relationships we had as a young person and with any group that had an impact on us or that we identify with. To develop the self-awareness that is so important to minimize the effects of bias on our decisions, we need to better understand the elements defining our group culture. National culture generally has an important impact on our personality development since we tend to be immersed in a cultural soup of social media, news

---

169   Eric Luis Uhlmann, Victoria L. Brescoll, and Elizabeth Levy Paluck, "Are Members of Low Status Groups Perceived as Bad, or Badly Off? Egalitarian Negative Associations and Automatic Prejudice," *Journal of Experimental Social Psychology* 42, no. 4 (2006): 491–499.

interpretations, education, friends and family. Even language, climate, and geography could be tied to our principal culture.

Another reason national culture is relevant to us as leaders is motivation. Our desire to fulfill a need triggers a series of behaviors to meet that need. For example, if I am thirsty, I go to the kitchen, get a glass, fill it with water, and drink it.[170] In simple words, a trigger (antecedent) results in an action (behavior) that is reinforced, neutralized, or punished by a consequence. The motivation or trigger occurs when there is a gap between the desired state and the actual state that pushes us to act to close that gap. This information came from the research conducted in the 1950s and '60s by a gentleman named David McClelland, who developed the theory of Learned Needs (aka Motivation Need theory).

This theory states that four levels govern our motivation: (1) the need for achievement, (2) the need for affiliation, (3) the need for power, and (4) the need for uniqueness.[171] As you may imagine, these four needs are culturally defined. For example, the need for uniqueness, or differentiating oneself from others, may not apply as much in a collective type of culture (i.e., China, Mexico) where you put the needs of the larger community before your own. Still, in a 1976 study published in the *Harvard Business Review*, McClelland, collaborating with Burnham,[172] argued that those needs affected the management style of organizational leaders. The researches drew connections between an individual's dominating need and her leadership preference. For example, an affiliative manager that sought to be

---

170 Todd Donavan, Michael Minor, and John Mowen, *Consumer Behavior* (McGraw-Hill, 2014).

171 George M. Zinkhan, Margy Conchar, Ajay Gupta, and Gary Geissler, "Motivations Underlying the Creation of Personal Web Pages: an Exploratory Study," *Advances in Consumer Research* 26 (1999).

172 David C. McClelland and David H. Burnham, "Power Is the Great Motivator," *Harvard Business Review* 73, no. 1 (1995): 126–139.

liked above all (strong affiliation need) and the institutional manager whose focus was to gain and exercise power.

As an international business executive, two of my preferred profiling tools are Hofstede's Cultural Compass,™ (https://www.hof-stede-insights.com/product/culture-compass/) and Meyer's Culture Map (https://www.erinmeyer.com/tools/). Both tools provide leaders with a profile of their preferences for different attributes. The tools are backed up by independent research and are easy to comprehend. Hofstede's tool also comes with a narrative that includes potential challenges to watch for, as well as potential advantages when interacting with an individual from another national culture. Word of advice though—except for your results, the national profiles are based on averages from consolidated information and, therefore, should be taken as a "most likely" scenario but not the absolute truth. As Sherlock Holmes once said in *The Sign of Four* (Sir Arthur Conan Doyle): "While the individual man is an insoluble puzzle, in the aggregate he becomes a mathematical certainty." In these culture profile assessments, you are looking at aggregated results of national culture.

Before we dive into the specifics of these tools, it is important to understand that the scales used here are on a continuum. We will be rated in each scale in relation to other culture. We also need to place ourselves in the other culture's mindset to truly understand how we will come across. Let me give you an example. If you ask a Chinese or Japanese executive how direct the communication style of an American executive is, they will tell you that Americans are very direct. Ask the same question of a Dutch or German, and they will tell you that the American executive is not very direct and uses too much flowery language. Who is right? All groups are right. The perspective on how direct or indirect that American executive is will be anchored in the groups' perspective. Dutch and German executives are at the higher end of the direct scale, while the Chinese and Japanese are at the other extreme of the scale, toward the indirect. At the same time, if you picture a continuous scale going from indirect to the left and direct to the right, American executives will be to the right of Chinese, and Japanese executives but to the left of the Dutch and German executives.

How communication styles are perceived could have repercussions on an individual's motivation. If your employees are Chinese, for example, and you are a Dutch manager, you may come across as direct and potentially rude and inharmonious. Spanish employees are very direct in most communication except for feedback—giving direct feedback to a Spaniard could have a demotivating effect and harm the relationship between the employee and the supervisor.

The other point to clarify about these two tools is that we are looking at averages. A few statistics here. Because the size of the groups assessed is very large (i.e., Hofstede started collecting data in 1972), the results are affected by the regression to the mean effect. This means that the extreme scores (highs and lows) of a large random sample are neutralized, extreme measurements are followed by moderate measurements, and the average for the group may not properly reflect the variance (differences) in the scores. Saying that American executives are direct does not mean that all American executives are direct. If you were to analyze the whole population, you would find American executives that are far from the American Executive Average at either side of the spectrum. On average, though, the population of the American executives will tend to be more toward the right side, or the direct side of the spectrum.

Hofstede´s Cultural Compass™

Hofstede´s Cultural Compass™ compares an individual´s cultural profile against his own country of origin, the cultural profile of the host country, and a list of cultures from potentially similar countries as well as significantly different ones. This report asks for the participant's role in the host country. The assessment results involve the five culture dimensions drawn from Hofstede´s copious research on national culture over the last four decades.[173] Those dimensions are (1) power distance, or the perception of power distribution within an organization or institutions; (2) uncertainty avoidance or society´s tolerance for ambiguity, uncertainty and the anxiety produced (or not) by that environmental ambiguity; (3) masculinity versus femininity or the preference of specific gender roles, which affect an individual's behavior (force versus nurturing); (4) individualism versus collectivism, or the independence or interdependence (being part of a larger whole); and (5) short- versus long-term orientation, or the tolerance for change and individual resilience.

Meyer´s Culture Map

Erin Meyer developed her tool based on the existing theories of Edward Hall, Geert Hofstede, Robert House, and Mansour Javidan and consolidated them with her research conducted over the last decade through her executive program at INSEAD.[174] This assessment involves a two-step process (https://www.erinmeyer.com/tools/the-personal-bundle-solution/). First, the executive is asked to complete a personal assessment that will determine her cultural

---

173 Geert Hofstede, *Cultures and Organizations: Software of the Mind: Intercultural Cooperation and its Importance* (McGraw-Hill, 2010); Geert Hofstede, Bram Neuijen, Denise Daval Ohayv, and Geert Sanders, "Measuring Organizational Cultures: a Qualitative and Quantitative Study across Twenty Cases," *Administrative Science Quarterly* (1990): 286–316.

174 Erin Meyer, *The Culture Map: Breaking through the Invisible Boundaries of Global Business* (Public Affairs, 2014).

map. Then, she will have the opportunity to choose from a list of the applicable countries and see how she compares to the aggregate results of other executive participants from the chosen countries. Currently, the Culture Map includes information on sixty-five countries. The resulting culture map provides a visualization of her cultural profile compared to that of the countries of interest and is based on eight dimensions—communicating (low context versus high context), evaluating (direct negative feedback versus indirect negative feedback), persuading (concept-first versus application-first), leading (egalitarian versus hierarchical approach), deciding (consensual versus top-down), trusting (task-based versus relationship-based), disagreeing (confrontational versus avoids confrontations), and scheduling (linear time versus flexible time).

The visual representation allows the executive to identify potential gaps in cultural preferences. For example, if she looks at the evaluating dimension and her scores are closer to the direct negative feedback, meaning that she wants frank, timely, and direct negative feedback but is dealing with a Spaniard that has a preference for indirect negative feedback, she should adjust her feedback style to be culturally-sensitive and effective. Let's not forget that during communication, if we elicit a strong negative emotion, the amygdala will kick in in our listener, triggering the fight-flight-freeze survival response and hence, our message will get lost in the emotional reaction. If the message is lost, then the reader will intuit that any desired future behavioral adjustments will be missed.

In our VUCA world, leaders need to develop cultural understanding to improve their interactions with the organization's diverse stakeholders. The self-administration of the cultural intelligence scales (ECQS), the implicit association test (IAT), the intercultural effectiveness scale (IES), and the cultural profiling assessments previously presented will contribute to a robust, conscious knowledge base of a leader's potential cultural hijackers. This level of cultural self-awareness will improve bilateral, or two-party, communication, improving the chances for a successful outcome between them.

TRIGGERING BIASES IN OTHERS

Managing the Perceptions We Project

Most of the research that I have read over the last ten years has pointed to four main factors for successful leaders. First, the obvious—our achievement is based on the skills we have acquired over the years, either through education, experience (successes and failures), or critical thinking. The second factor can be traced to one´s network of friends, colleagues, and other connections. Networking is a vital activity for any leader and strongly correlates with a leader's access to information and growth opportunities. The third and fourth factors are the topic of this chapter and revolve around likability and political savviness, which I summarize as executive presence.

On the likability side, many studies point to a certain correlation with physical factors. For example, research finds that taller people are perceived as having a better chance of success than shorter people,[175] the skin tone of African Americans may affect favorability during the hiring and promotion processes,[176] and skinnier and sportier individuals are perceived as better leaders.[177] However, likability is mostly connected to our personality and reputation. Reputation is especially important because it relates to the way people perceive us and affects people's reactions to our decisions.

---

175 Timothy A. Judge and Daniel M. Cable, "The Effect of Physical Height on Workplace Success and Income: Preliminary Test of a Theoretical Model," *Journal of Applied Psychology* 89, no. 3 (2004): 428.

176 Matthew S. Harrison and Kecia M. Thomas, "The Hidden Prejudice in Selection: a Research Investigation on Skin Color Bias," *Journal of Applied Social Psychology* 39, no. 1 (2009): 134–168.

177 Kerry S. O'Brien, Janet D. Latner, Daria Ebneter, and Jackie A. Hunter, "Obesity Discrimination: the Role of Physical Appearance, Personal Ideology, and Anti-Fat Prejudice," *International Journal of Obesity* 37, no. 3 (2013): 455.

Political savviness goes beyond our ability to make new connections. To be politically savvy implies that we understand the coalitions that exist around us. We know how to interact effectively with the members of those coalitions, and we have an understanding of how corporate politics will affect different decisions in the workplace. Likability and political savviness help define one's executive presence.

The ability to form a quick impression of others is a human survival tool. Our brain is wired to detect dangers as much as it is to maximize rewards. Remember what I mentioned before—when faced with an unknown individual, our brains race to classify the individual as belonging to in- or out-group. Remember we previously talked about classifying individuals as a friend or a foe? Let me explain the physiological reasons behind that behavior. Our brains are aroused by potential behaviors or events that it might consider dangerous by activating our "reptilian" brain, or the limbic system, which includes our hippocampus and amygdala, two of the most ancient (evolutionarily speaking) part of our brains. The limbic system activates an array of hormones to get us ready for the fight-flight-freeze or appease reactions. For instance, when an individual approaches, we immediately fight the ambiguity and uncertainty of the situation by classifying that individual as a friend or foe, with foe being the default choice.[178] This reaction is part of our success to adapt and survive different scenarios.

In organizational environment, that first impression that would propel us into one of the categories (friend or foe) could be better manage by developing our executive presence. The Center for Talent Innovation defined executive presence as the combination of

---

178   David Rock, "Managing with the Brain in Mind," Oxford Leadership, 2009, http://www.oxfordleadership.com/wp-content/uploads/2016/08/oxford-leadership-article-managing-with-brain-in-mind.pdf.

gravitas, communication, and appearance.[179] Their research found that gravitas is defined by behaviors showing confidence, integrity, decisiveness, emotional intelligence, reputation, and visionary qualities. Communication involves the ability to command a room with passion and charisma. Finally, appearance acts as a conduit for gravitas and communication—how we look can either help or hinder our message. Good grooming and physical attractiveness, both very culturally dependent, were identified as key to a positive appearance.

Looking at overall executive presence, how quickly do we judge people? In a 2018 article published in the journal *Proceedings of the National Academy of Sciences*, researchers found that we make decisions about people's personalities based on facial appearances within a few hundred milliseconds.[180] Their findings documented that the individual's face (looks and appearances) and our own assumptions shape our first impressions. Jonathan Freeman, one of the lead researchers for that article, explained that "initial impressions of faces can bias how we interact and make critical decisions about people, and so understanding the mechanisms behind these impressions is important for developing techniques to reduce biases based on facial features that typically operate outside of awareness."[181]

As a college instructor, I found the following study even more terrifying. According to Ambady and Rosenthal, college students' first impressions of a professor after being exposed to a short silent video clip were correlated to that professor's end-of-semester

179 Sylvia Ann Hewlett, Lauren Leader-Chivée, Laura Sherbin, Joanne Gordon, and Fabiola Dieudonné, "Executive Presence, Key Findings" (New York: Center for Talent Innovation, 2013).

180 Stolier, Ryan M., Eric Hehman, Matthias D. Keller, Mirella Walker, and Jonathan B. Freeman. "The conceptual structure of face impressions." *Proceedings of the National Academy of Sciences* 115, no. 37 (2018): 9210-9215.

181 James Devitt-Nyu, "Ideas about Personality Skew How We Judge Faces," *Futurity*, August 27, 2018, https://www.futurity.org/personality-how-we-judge-faces-1847602/.

evaluations.[182] Just by observing a teacher's behaviors for less than two hundred fifty milliseconds, the student had already developed a perception about that teacher's performance. While the study does not expand on the potential reasons, I would speculate that cognitive dissonance played a role in the final evaluation; once the students had acquired a perception, they spent the rest of the semester justifying it by noting the teacher's behaviors that supported it and ignoring the ones that contradicted it. That study has definitely affected how I walk into a classroom on the first day of school.

Antonakis´s Charismatic Behaviors

We may think, *how is that relevant to me? After all, I am not a college professor but a leader.* The impact of our looks (what Antonakis called the "price tag around our neck"[183]) and how biases in other individuals may affect our reputation and success is evident in another example. In an experiment in Switzerland, researchers evaluated the correlation between the decision of voters and facial stereotypes. Antonakis and Dalgas tested 2,841 individuals, including 681 children, using a computer-simulated trip between two cities. The participant had to choose one of two faces as the captain of the boat, not knowing that those pictures shown were the winner and the runner-up of French Parliamentary elections. The study found a strong correlation between the children's choices for the captain and the winners of the elections. The participants were able to predict, with a high degree of accuracy, the winner simply by looking at the pictures of the two main candidates.

---

182 Nalini Ambady and Robert Rosenthal, "Half a Minute: Predicting Teacher Evaluations from Thin Slices of Nonverbal Behavior and Physical Attractiveness," *Journal of Personality and Social Psychology* 64, no. 3 (1993): 431.

183   John Antonakis, "Let's Face It: Charisma Matters," March 18, 2015, a TED Talk, https://youtu.be/SEDvD1IICfE

If charisma is that important, is it innate or can it be learned? Can a leader improve his charisma? Charisma results from the combination of the leader's actions and attributes.[184] Those actions and attributes evoke (or fail to evoke) motivation in followers. While affecting an individual's attributes could be difficult, a leader could affect followers' motivation by changing his behaviors. Studies show that appropriate training could have a significant effect on the perception and ratings of a leader's charisma.[185]

In an article published in the *Harvard Business Review* journal, Antonakis, Fenley, and Liechti summarized the results of their studies on the development of charisma through the Charismatic Leadership Tactics (CLT).[186] The researchers identified a series of tactics that could increase the perception of charisma among her followers. The list suggests the following actions:

Using metaphors, similes, and analogies to help listeners understand, relate to, and remember the message. Again, in our VUCA world, clarity is paramount for our success.

Using stories and anecdotes to engage the listener. Our brains are hard-wired to listen to stories allowing for cognitive connection between the storyteller and the audience. [187]

Using contrast to juxtapose our position with a competing point of view. Contrasting arguments through reason and passion

---

184   Robert J. House, "Weber and the Neo-Charismatic Leadership Paradigm: a Response to Beyer," *The Leadership Quarterly* 10, no. 4 (1999): 563–574.

185   John Antonakis, Marika Fenley, and Sue Liechti, "Can Charisma Be Taught? Tests of Two Interventions," *Academy of Management Learning and Education* 10, no. 3 (2011): 374–396.

186   John Antonakis, Marika Fenley, and Sue Liechti, "Learning Charisma. Transform Ourselves into the Person Others Want to Follow," *Harvard Business Review* 90, no. 6 (2012): 127–30.

187   Gary Adamson, Joe Pine, Tom Van Steenhoven, and Jodi Kroupa, "How Storytelling Can Drive Strategic Change," *Strategy and Leadership* 34, no. 1 (2006): 36–41; KenBurnett, *Storytelling Can Change the World* (The White Lion Press, 2014).

usually drive our point with the audience but also invites any divergent opinions.

Using rhetorical questions to actively engage the audience, encouraging individuals to consider different points of view and take a stand on the topic.

Using a three-part list to capture the listener's attention. Basically, support your point with three bullet points. Or create an antecedent-behavior-consequence sequence—if this trigger happens, this behavior occurs, and the consequence is such. Once a list is introduced, audiences will want to know the three items in the list to bring that point to a nice closure.

Showing integrity, credibility, authenticity, and passion to clearly manifest one's moral conviction and voicing those related sentiments to the audience.

Setting high (achievable) goals to inspire the audience. Goals should be part of the organizational vision we are implementing.

Using the right combination of voice tone, body, and facial expressions to engage the audience and denote passion for the topic of our presentation. While Mehrabian's original study that resulted in the 53/38/7 has been disputed[188], no expert will debate the importance of nonverbal communication. Facial expressions, tone of voice, and body language affect communication to a greater degree than the words we use. Subconsciously, our brains are programmed to read and interpret expressions, predisposing our interpretation of the words. Make sure that your nonverbal cues are aligned with your verbal cues by being authentic.

---

188 Albert Mehrabian, "Nonverbal Communication," *Nebraska Symposium on Motivation* (University of Nebraska Press, 1971).

Executive Presence

First, let me say that executive presence is a skill that can be learned and not a trait that we are either born with or not. Executive presence is about projecting confidence. It is about inspiring individuals to act and follow a vision. Our executive presence has an immediate effect on how others perceive us and affects our career growth and leadership effectiveness. It will activate the bias in others before we have a chance to engage in the conversation, as we have learned.

The concept of executive presence was researched in great depth by economist Sylvia Ann Hewlett, an expert on gender issues in the workplace. Based on the three characteristics of executive presence (gravitas, communication, and presence), first impressions could what the sun is to vampires. Some cultures teaches us to trust unless given a reason not to. In other cultures, trust needs to be earned. Still, we can improve the odds of our first impression by using the Charismatic Leadership Tactics we just reviewed.

In addition to working on our charismatic leadership tactics, Horth and his colleagues at the Center for Creative Leadership recommend developing our leadership brand. The leadership brand is a concept composed of two parts—the "I" now, in the present, and the aspirational "I," the "I" in the future.[189] Hopefully, we have a good idea on what type of leaders we are now and how we are perceived. The future leader, the aspirational "I", is the leader that we wish to become. Our leadership brand should also reflect our causes and values. That brand should be aligned with individuals´ expectations about our work, and our promises. When we act or stand for a certain position, we should be confirming our moral standing on the relevant issues.

---

189 David Magellan Horth, Lynn B. Miller, and Portia R. Mount, *Leadership Brand: Deliver on Our Promise* (Greensboro, NC: Center for Creative Leadership, 2016).

If our reputation does not truly reflect who we are as a leader, we need to manage that perception and make adjustments to transform it into the executive brand we wish to be known for, the truthful picture of who we are as a leader. Let's not forget that while we know our intent, we cannot guarantee how it will be received. Our intent and its outcome do not usually line up, but changing our behaviors with others can bring them into alignment.

We spoke before about how statistics might not have the results we were hoping for. We may show a person the facts supported by scientific research, and we expect that person to tell us, "You are right." How many times has that approach worked? Facts and data lack the emotional connection that most individuals require to change their views. We need to sell the facts as a story, tapping into the brain's hippocampus, relaying emotions. Marco Polo, the great explorer, said, "I speak, and I speak, but the listener retains only the words that he is expecting. It is not the voice that commands the story: it is the ear."

Think about my stats on immigration. Instead of going to all the data, I would need to first sell the emotions. For example, I am an immigrant myself. My dad told me once that even though I was born in Spain, "I was born with a Yankee soul." I moved to Michigan from Spain in the late 80s as an exchange student, and my love for this country grew exponentially as I met wonderful people. Before I completed my senior year in high school, I decided to go to a US college. I attended Central Michigan University where I received my bachelor's degree with majors in Human Resource Management, General Administration/International Business and Management, and Management Information Systems.

It was also there that I met my future wife. We moved to Glendale, Arizona, where I pursue my master's degree in International

Management from Thunderbird (The American Graduate School of International Management, now part of Arizona State University), and upon graduation, Nokia, a European company expanding into Latin America, hired me based on my education and language skills. The job took us to Texas, where my wife and I had four marvelous children, then to other international destinations such as China. I am grateful for all the opportunities that the United States has given me both personally and professionally. I have lived my dream life, married a wonderful, funny, and smart person, and had four intelligent and beautiful daughters that make me proud every day. I was able to pursue my passions for international business, multicultural management, and organizational psychology, growing successfully in my profession and fulfilling my love for developing present and future leaders.

I have had ample opportunities to give back to the community through volunteer work with educational organizations. My family and I strongly believe in contributing our time, our taxes, and our charitable donations. I have personally worked with law enforcement agencies to educate them on inclusion and diversity as well as to improve communication with the local community.

We are financially vested in our community through the acquisition of our homes (in four different states over the last three decades), and we hire local crews to make home improvements, buy local materials, and hire local services. Over that time, we have bought or leased many vehicles too. We have invested in putting our daughters through colleges in Colorado and Michigan. We have donated our time—over one hundred hours every year—food, clothes, furniture, and money to the Red Cross, the Catholic Church, the Discover Goodwill, and a long list of educational and health foundations. We have left a positive economic print in whatever city and state we happen to call home.

The day I became a US citizen was one of the happiest days of my life—a long dream come true. As an immigrant, I am grateful every day for the opportunities I have been offered, and I understand that this is a two-way relationship. We need to contribute and give back to this great nation to make it a bit better than when we found it. How am I as an immigrant a bad thing for this country?

What's your story?

CONCLUSION

The Swiss-born philosopher Jean-Jacques Rousseau believed that man was born innocent, and it was society that degraded his morals. Psychologist and behavioral economist Dan Ariely argued that people have an internal moral compass that prevents them from behaving badly. Of course, badly is defined by each individual in a different way. In his books, Ariely contended that we fudge certain facts to be able to misbehave in ways that we can rationalize, therefore, maintaining and defending our good moral righteousness.

Our environments and the people around us affect the rationalization of our misbehaviors. Social psychologists and developmental psychologists have argued about the age at which our morals—our moral compass—are set. While ages vary with the studies, twelve years old seems to be the average age for moral cementation, or the age at which our moral compass finds its north. By that age, we have usually developed a set of morals, values, beliefs, and norms that govern our behaviors and eventually affect our leadership style.

Those ideals are dictated to a great extent by our tribe and by the life experiences that mold our self-identities. While nature and genetics do play a role in determining our belief systems[190], it is my opinion that environmental causes, the nurture portion of our lives, have the most definite effect on that belief system.

Throughout this book, I aimed to convey the science behind our behaviors and thought processes as well as techniques to improve our effectiveness as leaders. A recent article from the Center for Creative Leadership best summarizes many of the concepts discussed over the last chapters. The study identified the fundamental four competencies for leaders. Those are (1) self-awareness, (2)

---

190 Hibbing, John R., Kevin B. Smith, and John R. Alford. *Predisposed: Liberals, conservatives, and the biology of political differences.* Routledge, 2013.

communication, (3) influence, and (4) learning agility.[191] You probably recognized those terms since we have learned about them throughout this book. Still, allow me to use those terms as I wrap up this work.

The first item, self-awareness, is a key element to developing and improving the effectiveness of our leadership styles in our multicultural world. It means knowing what makes us tick, knowing that there are things what we don´t know, knowing what assumptions we have, and how our belief system may be filtering external messages and how they affect our interpretations of those messages. We learned that we can develop our self-awareness through a series of assessments that rate our cultural intelligence, identify our biases, and our level of readiness to face new situations and new (volatile, uncertain, complex, and ambiguous) environments.

The great Chinese philosopher Confucius argued that if man could not correctly name what he was facing, and the language chosen was not in accordance to the truth of things, then he would fail in his endeavors. This is known as the rectification of names. By correctly labeling the biases we face in our daily lives, we move a step closer to our success as leaders. Regardless of one´s leadership style, there is abundant research supporting the importance of building a trustworthy relationship with other parties through effective communication. We should wonder if, as leaders, we can articulate our visions, our objectives, our goals, and our expectations from others. In a world of emails and remote peers, coworkers, and direct reports, we should be able to effectively communicate verbally and in writing.

---

191   "What Experienced Leaders Need to Know to Succeed," Center for Creative Leadership (website), https://www.ccl.org/articles/leading-effectively-articles/senior-level-trade-offs-what-experienced-leaders-need-to-know/.

To effectively communicate with anyone, we need to speak their language (literally and metaphorically); we need to understand the assumptions, beliefs, and norms that drive their behaviors; we need to understand the context affecting the individual such as the external contextual dimensions, organizational dimensions, and the national, regional, and tribal background of that individual; we need to understand the pressures that mold their demands and expectations for their leaders and themselves; in short, we need to check our assumptions at the door and see the person standing in front of us for who they are and not for whom we want them to be.

We took a quick dive into some motivational theories and how those motivations vary by employees. Needs play a significant role in motivating behaviors. The widening gap between a person's current state and their desired state gives rise to behaviors that can fill that gap. As leaders, we need to understand those individual needs and motivators to exert a positive influence on our teams, peers, customers, and stakeholders.

Cultural intelligence involves the ability to learn new things but also to reflect and expand on new information. Learning agility determines how well we learn from new situations, the use of our critical thinking to analyze and synthesize new information and apply it to new situations. The fact that you are reading this book already shows higher learning agility, your willingness to learn and understand biases, and how they affect your decision making and leadership style.

Awareness is a good start. This book provides you with tools to discover yourself as a leader and uncover areas that might require your attention. Just as self-awareness is important, an inclusive leader needs to develop and implement the systematic processes that will instill a culture of inclusiveness. That system requires the right climate and a psychologically safe environment to improve the teams' performance. It also involves an invitation to speak up and be heard. Finally, certain processes should be implemented as part of the overall design for inclusive culture, a type of fail-safe switch that would help neutralize biases.

To succeed in this VUCA world, we need to ensure we are making optimal use of all our assets, including our human capital. Inclusive leaders motivate employees to peak performance, driving productivity and profitability to new highs. Inclusively leading our diverse workforce does not only improve our organization's performance, but it makes our community and society a stronger one.

ABOUT THE AUTHOR

Dr. Juan M. Gallego has twenty plus years of experience in global business. He has held executive positions in the United States, Latin America, Europe, and China. As a consultant, he focuses on organizational development, culture awareness, inclusive leadership, and corporate executive training. His experience includes leading and facilitating projects in sales, strategy planning, organizational development, coaching, leadership development, and merger and acquisitions on a global level. He also facilitates diversity and inclusion workshops with law enforcement agencies and other organizations.

Dr. Gallego lectures about marketing and management at the University of Colorado (Colorado Springs) and facilitates executive workshops at the Center for Creative Leadership, a top-ranked global provider of leadership development. His education includes a Doctor of Psychology (Psy.D.) with a specialization in Organizational Consulting and a Master of International Management from Thunderbird School of Global Management.